P9-EGM-741

Radical Kindness

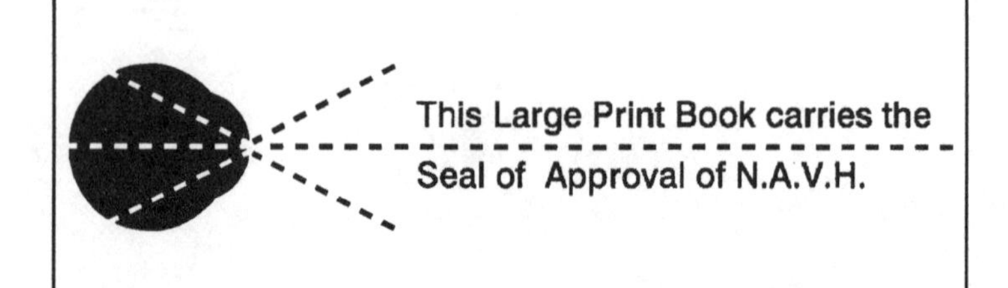
This Large Print Book carries the
Seal of Approval of N.A.V.H.

Radical Kindness

The Life-Changing Power of Giving and Receiving

Angela C. Santomero

Foreword by Deepak Chopra

THORNDIKE PRESS
A part of Gale, a Cengage Company

Farmington Hills, Mich • San Francisco • New York • Waterville, Maine
Meriden, Conn • Mason, Ohio • Chicago

Thorndike Press, a part of Gale, a Cengage Company.

Thorndike Press® Large Print Lifestyles.
The text of this Large Print edition is unabridged.
Other aspects of the book may vary from the original edition.
Set in 16 pt. Plantin.

**LIBRARY OF CONGRESS CIP DATA ON FILE.
CATALOGUING IN PUBLICATION FOR THIS BOOK
IS AVAILABLE FROM THE LIBRARY OF CONGRESS**

ISBN-13: 978-1-4328-6598-6 (hardcover alk. paper)

Published in 2019 by arrangement with HarperWave, an imprint of HarperCollins Publishers

Printed in Mexico
1 2 3 4 5 6 7 23 22 21 20 19

This book is dedicated to YOU, the READER, and to those special people who inspire you, each and every day, to be radically kind. By choosing kindness, you change the world. Thank you.
#RadicalKindness

CONTENTS

II. BE KIND TO YOURSELF

III. BE KIND TO OTHERS

FOREWORD

We live in a world where kindness is in short supply and seems to be getting scarcer every day. Yet no matter how much the supply dwindles, it is endlessly renewable. If we want to change reality, we must begin with this assurance: Kindness, along with its close companions empathy, compassion, and love, is an aspect of consciousness that cannot be created or destroyed. It can only be forgotten and rediscovered.

Once they begin to accept that assurance, people can begin to transform their lives by reminding themselves that the body and mind have an infinite capacity for change and renewal. At the heart of this understanding is the need to cultivate a greater self-awareness. Knowing who we really are — the product of consciousness creating without limits — drastically changes the choices we make. When we realize that we are connected to a field of infinite potential, we have a reliable source for transformation, not just personally but in society at large. Kindness assumes great importance after it is aligned with a great purpose — revitalizing, nourishing, and healing our lives.

Angela Santomero's deeply insightful *Radical Kindness* can help us grow in the all-important area of self-awareness. Her work is not only an inspiring guide to self-transformation, but it offers the practical means for experiencing what can be called kindness consciousness. The journey begins by paying attention to the need for inner and outer peace, for leading our daily lives from a place of deep-seated benevolence and thoughtfulness, especially toward ourselves.

Self-care has become a popular theme in recent years, but it raises in some people the shadow of self-centeredness. For them, self-care is merely a glossy repackaging of the old axiom about looking out for number one. Being kind to yourself can sound like a selfish pursuit. Shouldn't kindness be something we offer others? Yes, of course. However, self-care is a necessary ingredient to a happy and purposeful life. Unless we love and treat *ourselves* well, we are ill-equipped to do the same for others. The Golden Rule, a philosophy shared by most cultures around the world in one form or another, urges us to love our neighbors *as we love ourselves.*

Yet as simple and enduring as this teaching is, human nature blocks the way. Driven by the endless demands of "I, me, and mine," we are constantly pressured to act out of narrow self-interest first and foremost. We can have the best intentions to do to others as we would have them do to us, but somehow self-interest keeps postponing the day when it actually happens. I think the only answer is to find a level of consciousness that goes beyond self-interest. Kindness cannot be measured or quantified; therefore, doling it out erratically and in small doses doesn't get at the heart of the matter.

The ego personality has a secret side that must be exposed to light. The ego's public side is all about getting pleasure and avoiding pain, accumulating money and the good things it buys, and rising in the world, generally. But in its secret self, the ego knows that all of its demands and desires are based on a fearful insecurity. "I" fills a hole, a void of true meaning and fulfillment. True meaning and fulfillment cannot come and go. Things that come and go fuel insecurity and anxiety. We grip tightest to what we fear to lose. Therefore, living according to "I, me, mine" is a defensive posture, no matter how well life is going on the surface.

In this collective addiction to defending our self-interest from everyone else who is defending their self-interest, we accept a falsehood. Life isn't based on the foibles of human nature; the void we fear inside is self-created. Nothing about insecurity, anxiety, and lack is destined to exist — all of these things are born of judgment against the self. Once you see the situation and want to remedy it, self-care assumes its proper purpose; it heals all judgment against the self.

We can truly love one another once we love who we are. The ego-personality is stubborn and well established. It knows how to use acts of kindness as addons to its agenda rather than as expressions of the true self that transcends ego. It knows how to co-opt our best intentions. It will seize upon any negative experience to make us scurry back to a place of safety, which to the ego is a very selfish place. I'm not discouraged by such obstacles but bring them up to underscore what we need to do, which isn't to attack our sense of insecurity and lack — attacking the shadow side of the ego only makes it more defensive.

A better approach is to treat ourselves with compassion, honesty, and patience. Too many of the travesties and destructive trends in the world exist because human beings don't recognize the proper way to love themselves. *We mistreat the "other" so that the sad truth about ourselves can be deflected. That's the vicious circle that Radical Kindness breaks, beginning with each individual who is willing to wake up to higher reality.*

Higher reality is always inward. Deliberately living from a place of Radical Kindness means living from a place of positive mental and emotional change. When you begin to understand more deeply the true power of love and understanding, you discover that change and renewal are natural — putting up obstacles and defenses are the essence of what is unnatural. Reality unfolds here and now, which is the only place it could unfold. There is no map for locating the here and now, but we're all equipped to find where it is. The here and now has its own sense of presence. I'd describe this presence through feelings of openness, curiosity, creative imagination, receptivity, allowing, appreciation, inner quiet, and great alertness.

The ego can simulate those

things. It can even achieve them in a hit-and-miss fashion. But these are not mental constructs to be toyed with. They are the traits of the true self once a person has experienced the reality of higher consciousness. In a word, they come as one package. Compassion and kindness are part of the same package. They emerge in the presence of the here and now. You don't struggle to find them but instead allow a natural, effortless unfolding from the inside.

Over the last few years, science has begun to see that changing the way we think can alter the brain in powerful ways. This leads to new ways of experiencing the heights of who we can be. The equation is simple: cultivating self-awareness by living as best as we can in the present moment leads to changes in energy, which leads to changes in the mind and body. The process is self-reinforcing. The more you open yourself to the here and now, the greater your realization of what emerges from the field of all possibilities. We can call this the dual role of healer and healed coming together as one. By focusing our attention on being kind to ourselves, by projecting compassion and peace inwardly, we alter how we react to the world outwardly. When this process is truly whole and not ego-driven, the world responds in a similar fashion.

Radical Kindness is an important

antidote to the poisonous times we are living in, and we can't look to others to remedy things for us. Radical Kindness begins with you. Realizing this has enough energy to revolutionize the way you live. Let Angela's book help you to see how.

— DEEPAK CHOPRA

Mister Rogers Saw Me: A definition of Radical Kindness

When I was four years old, I looked forward every day to visiting my friend Mister Rogers. As soon as my mother turned on that television set, I couldn't take my eyes off his smiling, loving face. Something about the way he spoke — so slowly, clearly, patiently — made me feel that he had all the time in the world for me.

I grew up in a chaotic Italian

American household, where everyone was passionately loud and always rushing from one thing to another. And while I had loving parents, they were often busy doing what grown-ups do: working, cooking, eating, cleaning up, sleeping. But as I watched Mister Rogers walk through that door, hang up his blazer, put on his cardigan, and change into his sneakers, all the noise of the outside world seemed to disappear. For half an hour every day, I felt *seen.* Mister Rogers paid attention to me. He spoke lovingly and compassionately. And as I looked back at him through the glass of that TV screen, I really believed he could *see me.*

Of course, I know Mister Rogers

didn't *literally* see me through the television screen. Even so, he was able to connect with me and millions of other children in a way that few others ever have. That's because Mister Rogers practiced something I've come to call radical kindness.

With his soft-spoken demeanor, Fred Rogers was the antithesis of what we typically think of as "radical." Yet I'm using the word's original meaning. The term *radical* comes from the Latin word for "root." And indeed, Fred Rogers placed kindness at the root of all he said and did on *Mister Rogers' Neighborhood,* a program that began in 1968, a time of social and cultural upheaval in the United

States. With a contentious war being waged in Vietnam and violent clashes over civil rights at home, Mister Rogers treated all children and adults who tuned in to his show or who visited his make-believe neighborhood with tenderness, consideration, respect, patience, and empathy, and that's something that could rightly be called radical or even revolutionary, in a period mired in discord. Kindness was at the root of all he did and said.

I wrote this book because we are all suffering from a shortage of kindness, and it just might be time for a new revolution, for radical change. We're impatient with others. We've stopped listening to voices we don't agree with, especially when it comes to hot-button topics such as politics, religion, and parenting. We're even unkind to ourselves. We don't get enough sleep, we don't eat right, we take on more responsibility than we can handle, and our self-talk (i.e., the endless self-criticism in our heads) leaves much to be desired.

Following in Fred Rogers's footsteps, I've tried in my own way to bring a little love into the world, by creating PBS's *Daniel Tiger's Neighborhood,* which teaches children the value of kindness, the importance of building a strong character, and the need for integrity and compassion. This book, in turn, was inspired in many ways by my experiences in children's television, which have forced me to get back to basics and remind myself what kindness is and why it matters in the world. And while the show I created is admittedly for the young among us, its lessons are ones we could all stand to be reminded of.

What is kindness, exactly? It's such a simple concept, yet one that begs to be reconsidered. To me, kindness is seeing with one's heart rather than one's head, which leads to interacting with and responding to others with compassion, rather than misunderstanding them. Kindness is about increasing our awareness of how we see and, consequently, treat ourselves and others.

Practicing radical kindness reminds us of what is essential in our own lives: our families, our work, our friendships, our communities. It helps us see every man, woman, and child we meet the way Mister Rogers did: as individuals possessing great richness, as embodiments of love.

In the pages that follow, I will share a number of strategies and practices for seeing more clearly with your heart. We will do this in four parts: by defining kindness through heart-seeing; and by examining and experimenting with kindness first to ourselves, then to others, and finally, to the world.

Practicing kindness may sound like a simple proposition, but the implications of it are anything but. Being kind to yourself is a gift of strength; it can give you purpose and a deep sense of joy about your life. Being kind to others is a gift of compassion; it can build the self-image and confidence of a fellow human being. Being kind to the world is a gift of hope and awareness; it involves cultivating an active social conscience. These new ways of interacting with yourself, other people, and the world at large are, in essence, your gifts to the future. Your acts of kindness can have a lasting impact on people and the communities in which they live. By merely practicing kindness, you can contribute to preserving the home we all share and even potentially affect the ways nations interact, by doing your small part to shift public focus away from aggression and toward peace, tolerance, and compassion for other people, other cultures, and the planet itself.

Yes, these are big claims (I'll go into them in greater detail later), and as with things that require introspection and change, there is a learning curve. But the journey to radical kindness starts with you, for you are a world unto yourself. Plant that first seed of kindness within, tend to it, feed it — give it strong *roots* — and it will grow into a garden that can spread far beyond the boundaries of your own life.

■ ■ ■ ■

I.
What is Radical Kindness?

■ ■ ■ ■

1
Heart-Seeing

The First Step Toward Radical Kindness

Mister Rogers once said, "There are three ways to ultimate success: The first way is to be kind. The second way is to be kind. The third way is to be kind." I'd like to think that we all know what it means to be kind to one another. It's saying thank you, holding the door open for someone, feeding a stray cat, or comforting a loved one after a bad day at home, work, or school. It's what happens every time you're told to "be nice," and one of the first concepts introduced to children in preschool and kindergarten. Even the most downtrodden members of society know about kindness, if only because they are painfully aware of the lack of it in their own lives.

But what do we mean by *radical* kindness? Radical kindness means rooting all you say and do in kindness, being unconditionally kind all the time, to everyone. It means going beyond situational niceness or merely "doing the right thing" and, instead, living from a place of compassion.

WHAT IS HEART-SEEING?

As Antoine de Saint-Exupéry writes in *The Little Prince,* "It is only with the heart that one can see rightly; what is essential is invisible to the eye."* When you are a radically kind person, you "see" with your heart. Seeing with our hearts offers us an opportunity to make what is often invisible visible. When we "heart-see," we see through a lens of trust, respect, love, patience, and warmth. Heart-seeing connects us to something that is so beautiful, so transformative, that the world before us changes in delightful, unexpected, even revolutionary

* Antoine de Saint-Exupéry, *The Little Prince,* trans. Katherine Woods (New York: Harcourt, Brace & World, 1943).

ways.

As Dr. Wayne Dyer said in his *Power of Intention* PBS special, "When you change the way you look at things, the things you look at change."* When that inner change happens, when we embrace and understand the importance of kindness, we can transform our inner lives and the outer world. We feel better; we're less anxious and more creative; we have more energy; and when we look at people, we see them in a more accepting way.

When you heart-see, you interpret

* Dr. Wayne Dyer, *The Power of Intention* (Carlsbad, CA: Hay House, 2004), 249; available for viewing at https://www.youtube.com/watch?v=urQPraeeY0w.

what you think you are observing with a keen awareness that you cannot possibly know the whole story of someone else's life. That rude waiter? Well, you don't know what kind of day he's been having — maybe someone was unkind to him; maybe dozens of people were, and he just wants to go home. That baby screaming on the plane? Sure, she's annoying, but maybe that child hasn't slept all day and has a headache. Unlike you and me, the baby can't tell her parents what's bothering her.

Practicing radical kindness means assuming the best of everyone — heart-seeing them — and then acting toward them with compassion, patience, and humility. It means infusing what we think, say, and do throughout the day with warmth, understanding, and care. It means treating everyone — including ourselves! — as important, as if they matter in the world. And yes, that means *everyone,* whether that person is a family member, friend, stranger, panhandler, someone with opposing political views, or the loudmouth on his cell phone in a hushed coffee shop. To see all human beings *first* with unconditional compassion is to heart-see them, and it is the only way to integrate a practice of radical kindness into our lives.

Yes, living a life of radical kindness challenges that old idea that nice guys finish last or that compassion is somehow a form of weakness. Research has demonstrated time and again that you can be kind *and* strong, compassionate *and* determined, gentle *and* opinionated. Seeing with the heart takes guts, and acting with compassion takes self-confidence and perspective. The qualities you need in order to be kind (compassion, integrity, respect) are exactly the same qualities you need to be brave, strong, and successful.

To practice radical kindness by heart-seeing is to practice the art of noticing. Becoming more aware of others, becoming more sensitive, necessitates that we first notice our own circumstances, needs, and qualities. (We'll come back to this idea and discuss it further in chapters to come.) Then, as we move beyond our own personal needs to see the concerns, heartbreaks, and struggles of others, we widen our vision of the world. Too often we get so caught up in our day-to-day struggles that we don't realize that the person standing next to us on line at the grocery store is having a bad day or is worried about a sick parent, or the kid behind the counter at the fast-food restaurant is in need of a few words of gratitude.

Try On Someone Else's Shoes

One of the ways we can become more sensitive to the needs of others is to imagine ourselves or someone we love in their position. Reflect for a moment: Would you want your overtired mother to have to work the night shift at that hospital when she desperately needs a good night's sleep? Would you want your son to be unnoticed and unappreciated in a minimum-wage job he works while carrying a full load of college courses?

Broadening our awareness beyond ourselves to include everyone and everything around us can seem like hard work, especially for those who have a grudge against another, who haven't had their morning cup of coffee, or who are irritable by nature. Still, the rewards of heart-seeing — the physical, mental, emotional, and psychological rewards — are worth the effort.

We need only retrain our eyes to look past the surface, to see people for who they truly are. We need only tune our ears to hear not just their words but also the emotion, the intent, the sorrow, or the loneliness behind those words. We need only prod our minds to become more actively engaged in the thoughts we entertain about what we see and hear.

The more we consciously choose kindness over criticism or animosity, the more we develop the "kindness muscles" that give us the strength to deal with life in an effective, joyful way.

Creating Beauty Through Heart-Seeing

Imagine what the world would be like if we all chose to see with our hearts, to lead with kindness. There would be fewer family conflicts, more harmony at work, a greater sense of community in our towns and cities, more peace in general, at every level, from the internal to the international. We would all feel lighter in the things we did because we wouldn't be carrying around the burden of stress that comes from judging or trying to control others — the kind of stress that ages people, drains them of energy.

While the world often seems chaotic and harsh, there are kind people out there. They may not advertise it, but they are out there just the same. Watch for them. See how they live. Pay attention to what they do. Most people can think of a teacher or a friend who always goes that extra mile to make someone feel welcome, often with nothing more than a handshake or a warm smile that says, "I'm glad you're here." Remember those people and how they made you feel — the stranger holding the door for you; the driver on the freeway who, with a smile and a wave, let you cut in; the person who said, "Good morning!" as you passed by — take those moments, notice them, consider their power, and use them as building blocks as you begin to develop your own practice of radical kindness. Recognize that the way others "heart-see" can inform and expand your vision of what being radically kind looks like in the world.

Cultivating heart-seeing, developing a kind outlook and mind-set, and making kindness an intentional part of your daily life can be a counterbalance to some of the negativity we all encounter each day.

When What We See Is Unkind

The Indian yogi Paramahansa Yogananda once articulately wrote in his *Spiritual Diary,* "Let the ugliness of unkindness to others impel me to make myself beautiful with loving-kindness. May harsh speech from my companions remind me to use sweet words always. If stones from evil minds are cast at me, let me send in return only missiles of goodwill."*

In other words, sometimes we find inspiration for kind actions by noticing what is going on around us that we *don't* like. If you don't appreciate a boss's condescending tone, make a conscious effort *not* to treat your coworkers or direct reports the same way. If your spouse snaps at you after a stressful day, notice how that makes you feel and then use that experience

* Paramahansa Yogananda, *Spiritual Diary: An Inspirational Thought for Each Day of the Year*, 2nd ed. (Self-Realization Fellowship, 2005).

to tailor your words toward kindness when the kids are giving you a hard time. In effect, find ways to live by the Golden Rule, to treat others as you would want them to treat you.

Heart-Seeing 101

In order to practice radical kindness, you first have to be proficient at heart-seeing. Start your practice here, with the following steps:

- *Practice heart-seeing yourself.* Think of one thing you love about yourself. Look past your inner critic to your best intrinsic quality and then appreciate it for the great gift it truly is. Maybe you are exceptionally nurturing. Maybe you have a terrific ability to withhold judgment, which makes you a great listener. Maybe someone who is in despair would love to have a piece of your staunch optimism. Maybe your patience enables you to help kids who need a calm, composed, unflappable adult in their life. If you aren't sure what your best intrinsic qualities are, ask a good friend or family member what *they* think they are. Once you have your best qualities in mind, allow yourself the pleasure of feeling good about them, even proud. This is heart-seeing yourself. Again, heart-seeing yourself is preparation for becoming better at heart-seeing others.

- *Practice heart-seeing friends and family.* It can sometimes be easy to take for granted the people we care about the most in our lives. We can fall into a rut, in the way we listen and react to those around us, often because we are so busy, distracted, or simply not paying attention to things that are familiar. A child might start to talk to his mother about a fellow classmate who is annoying him, but she only half listens because she is trying to make dinner. A mom calls her son and wants to talk, but he is running around town doing errands and doesn't really give her the attention she craves from him. To practice heart-seeing with our family and friends, the first thing we can do is slow down, then stop, then look and listen with focus and intention, as if for the first time — as if they were not familiar. Does it really matter if dinner is a few minutes late? Will it be the end of the world if that trip to the grocery store gets delayed an hour so you can be present for someone who cares for you and needs you? This often requires a slight shift in priorities, and that can come down to a single moment in which we ask ourselves: What is really important right now?

- *Practice heart-seeing the world.* When we think about kindness, we might not first think about how we can be compassionate and loving to the world at large. Radical kindness to the world starts with paying attention to how you see the world around you. What do you notice about the people who are outside your circle of family and friends, the people you know *of* but do not know personally? What do you see when people around you are different from you or speak a different language?

Later, we will dig in to explore ways to heart-see, act toward, and interact with those people beyond your immediate circle, the people you don't know, and the implications of kind acts for the world and the future. But today, start *noticing* your general attitudes. Sometimes all you have to do is pay attention to your own thoughts and feelings, and a whole new world of understanding will open up for you.

2
First See, Then Act

Radical Kindness Means Action, Not Reaction

If radical kindness begins with taking a fresh view of yourself, others, and the world, the next step is to act upon what you've seen with your heart. When you see more deeply into yourself and others, your actions will become more compassionate, especially when you begin to notice the difference between what it means to react and what it means to act. Heart-seeing, therefore, can be the catalyst that helps turn unkind reaction into kind action.

If you typically follow your knee-jerk reactions when people do things you don't like, you may think that's your nature. It's not. It's a habit. Our brains are wired to create habitual ways of thinking, patterns that keep us from getting lost or forgetting how to perform a task, that remind us who our friends are. But sometimes we develop habits that aren't in our best interest. Think of biting your nails or reaching for your smartphone whenever you feel bored. The good news is you can rewire your brain, reset your conditioning, by pivoting away from a negative reaction, focusing on the sensations you're experiencing inside, and then consciously choosing a kinder action. It takes awareness, time, and patience, but it can be done.

When we see with our hearts, we get better at responding to people, to our surroundings, to novelty, disappointment, frustration, and conflict — we listen a little more closely, we give people a little more time. When we learn to be deliberate in our actions, to take our time, not to rush ourselves or others, it prepares us to handle difficulties in a more effective way.

Listen to Your "Heart-Brain"

For thousands of years, philosophers believed that the heart was the center of intelligence. In a 2013 *Huffington Post* article, psychologist Dr. Deborah Rozman reported that scientists had found that "the human heart, in addition to its other functions, actually possesses a heart-brain composed of about 40,000 neurons that can sense, feel, learn, and remember. The heart-brain sends messages to the head-brain about how the body feels and more." Rozman goes on to say that when we experience emotions, our heart's rhythm changes, and information is then sent throughout the body to the brain, changing us "neurologically, biochemically, biophysically, and energetically."* In other words, our emotional reactions have significant influence on our physical well-being.

Though we're not conscious of it, our heart-brain is constantly responding to positive and negative emotional stimuli.† One study from the University of New South Wales showed the effects of positive and negative emotional images on college students' ability to solve prob-

* Deborah Rozman, HeartMath LLC, "Let Your Heart Talk to Your Brain," updated December 6, 2017, https://www.huffpost.com/entry/ heart-wisdom_b_2615857.

† Galang Lufityanto et al., "Measuring Intuition: Nonconscious Emotional Information Boosts Decision Accuracy and Confidence," *Psychological Science* 27, no. 5 (2016): 622–34.

lems. For the study, the researchers showed a group of students an abstract array of moving dots and asked them to identify which way the dots were moving. Some students were exposed to subliminal emotional images while watching the dots, images flashed too quickly to be registered consciously, such as a cute puppy or a rearing snake. Others were not shown any images. The researchers were surprised to find that the students who were exposed to the emotional images, positive or negative, were better able to decide more accurately in which direction the cloud of dots was moving. They also made their decisions more quickly. Skin conductivity tests showed that heightened electrical impulses occurred in tandem with positive or negative reactions to the images, even though the students had *no conscious awareness* of those images. The researchers concluded that unconscious observation of images with emotional content boosted intuition, confirming earlier findings that intuition is a measurable phenomenon that improves reaction time and good decision making.

You may think you're not "seeing" anything deep when you look at someone with your heart, but this research suggests that your body registers emotional cues before you're even conscious of them. Perhaps, then, we should give emotions more credit for directing our behavior and value the influence they have on our decisions. Tuning in to our emotions in this way expands our vision of the situation at hand and tells us what a kind course of action might be.

Remember the Golden Rule

For instance, imagine you are in a grocery store on a Friday evening. You start down the cereal aisle, where you see a woman struggling with a toddler who is having a meltdown. The woman is flustered; her child, red-faced and screaming, is on the floor throwing a tantrum right in front of the Cheerios you need. You've had a long week, you're tired, and you just want to finish your shopping and get home. Even before you formulate a cogent thought, you're feeling annoyed. You might immediately tense up and may even express your annoyance by making a sour face.

But if you just pause and take a step back, allowing yourself to extend kindness toward the mother, you could turn the whole miserable situation around. Certainly, if you were in her shoes, you wouldn't want someone making matters worse by barreling down the aisle with a cartful of groceries and getting in the middle of an already difficult situation. Even if you're not a parent, you know what it's like to be tired and frustrated. Remember the Golden Rule: What would you want other people to do for you in a similar situation?

You might shoot the mother a commiserating glance, or say something consoling about how your kids used to do the same thing. Or you might just give her some space and time by retreating to another aisle. It doesn't matter if your actions are appreciated or even noticed. What matters is that you have overcome your first, critical reaction and replaced it with compassion. You have done the better thing. In fact, you've done the right thing.

Our actions don't have to be big or heroic. They can be as simple as a kind word, a hug, or keeping quiet while someone else talks to us about what they're feeling. Sometimes tiny acts can make a big difference in other people's lives — they can reverse a bad day or help someone feel wanted and important. And let's face it, we all want to feel important.

By increasing your awareness of what others are experiencing, you can learn to put kindness into daily action. And while of course you want to be kind to others, it is often best to start by looking inward. The first arena for radical kindness is ourselves, and that's just what the next chapters explore.

■ ■ ■ ■

II
Be Kind to Yourself

■ ■ ■ ■

3
Tune in to Glinda, Mute the Wicked Witch

Softening Your Inner Voice with Kindness

Each of us has a whole cast of characters inside our heads. For example, there's the worrier, the champion, the doubter, the do-gooder, the gossip, the nitpicker, and the one with anger management issues. I like to think of my inner voices as the cast of *The Wizard of Oz,* all skipping around inside my head, so let's use them as examples.

There is Glinda the Good Witch of the North, who approaches life with a jovial spirit and a desire to be kind and supportive: "You don't need to be helped any longer. You've always had the power to go back to Kansas."

There's the Wicked Witch of the West, who, when I try to escape a spiral of negative thinking, cackles, "Going so soon? I won't hear of it. My little party's just beginning!"

When I feel like a fraud, the Great Wizard of Oz booms, "Pay no attention to that woman behind the curtain!"

Like the Scarecrow, Tin Man, and Cowardly Lion, sometimes I feel brainless, heartless, or completely without courage; other times I feel smart, loving, and brave.

Dorothy gives me homegrown advice on the importance of family and home. But to be perfectly honest, most of the time I hear the high-pitched voices of the Munchkins, all talking at the same time, confusing me about which is the right way to Oz.

Often, we feel at the mercy of our inner voices. It can be hard to discern just who's talking and why. Sometimes one voice takes center stage, but a lot of the time, they all speak at once, creating a cacophony of noise, agitation, and anxiety. And I'm sure you don't need me to tell you how hard it can be to turn those voices off.

Muting the Wicked Witch . . .

The Wicked Witch can be one of the most difficult. She can be loud, screechy, critical, and just downright nasty. Her voice is the one that wants you to doubt yourself, that tells you that you aren't enough. She is your worst critic, the one who berates you for saying the wrong thing or not doing well enough on a test or at work, or for gaining weight, or for not seeing a problem a family member is having. When you have hopes and dreams, she tells you that you won't ever accomplish them, so why even try? It's the Wicked Witch who undermines your confidence and enumerates your faults. She can bring up feelings of guilt and shame about things that happened in your past — a bad breakup, the time you forgot your sister's birthday, that terrible thing you said to your mother. She's the one telling you you're selfish when you take time for yourself. The result? You're unkind to yourself. After all, the Wicked Witch has convinced you that unkindness is all you deserve.

. . . AND TUNING IN TO GLINDA

But we all have a Glinda voice, too, a voice that guides us gently, that listens carefully to our needs, and reminds us that we are worthy. She helps us focus our hearts and is the angel on our right shoulder countering the Wicked Witch on our left. Glinda dares you to dream big. She tells you what a good job you've done. She forgives you when you've made a mistake. She helps you reach inward and take care of yourself. Every time the Wicked Witch has something nasty to say, Glinda is there to offer support and optimism. She is your cheerleader. She reassures you that you can do it, that you've got this, that you're okay. Glinda is kind to you, and that's why she's the key to your being kind to yourself. She's the proof that you already know how to do this, if you can only drown out the voices that tell you that you don't deserve compassion.

You have the power to throw water on the Wicked Witch. You do this first by realizing that the harmful voices, the ones that try to tear you down and tear down others, are not you. Those hostile voices may be fears, disappointments, or unresolved issues from childhood, but you are more than those voices say you are. Learn to melt the Wicked Witch by dousing her with a bucket of kindness. You can listen to her rants for a time, but then kindly imagine Glinda waving a wand and saying, "Go away. You have no power here." Glinda is always there in the background, ready to step in. All you have to do is call on her, and that pretty glistening bubble will float into your consciousness (cue harp music), and Glinda will materialize. She is and always has been more powerful than the Wicked Witch. Why? Because Glinda embodies the power of love and joy, from which kindness originates. You should always take what the Wicked Witch says to you with a grain of salt. Sometimes, self-criticism can be a good thing, when it is correcting our own bad behavior, rather than who we are. But when the cranky green one is putting you down for the sake of shaming you, you can always choose Glinda's voice instead.

This can be more difficult on some days than others. When you're under stress or going through a rough patch in life, it's smart to give yourself a little bit of grace. When the Wicked Witch is especially loud, try this trick. Take fifteen minutes away from what you're doing and sit very still and listen. Don't try to shut out the voices. Don't try to make them go away. Just listen to the crazy. Try not to act on anything. Try not to judge. Let the voices have their say. Then, after that fifteen minutes, announce, "Time's up!" and go about your business. This simple meditation is a free shrink for all the voices inside your head. In time, believe it or not, those voices will get quieter and quieter.

(This strategy also works when dealing with people who intrude on your life with negativity — for example, a cranky coworker or someone who complains constantly, though never with constructive criticism. Ignoring such people is usually ineffective. A better way to deal with them is to give them a few minutes of "active listening." We'll talk more about active listening in the chapters ahead.)

Bottom line: Let the voices in your head have their say. Give them attention. Listen without judgment. Be supportive when necessary. Know that they inform you and that listening to them is in the service of heart-seeing yourself — *all* the parts of yourself. Listening to them is a simple form of meditation, really, one where you don't judge. You just notice. Let them speak. When you stop trying to suppress them, they usually move on.

You have the power to listen to whatever part of yourself will help you the most at any given moment. So, whenever the Wicked Witch rears her head, listen to her with the goodness and heart of a Glinda. Her kindness can break the noisy voices of self-doubt in your head and set you back on the Yellow Brick Road toward kindness. It works like magic. Really. Ask the Wizard.

4
Heart-See Yourself

Radical Kindness to Oneself

The fourteenth-century Persian poet Hafiz wrote, "I wish I could show you, when you are lonely or in darkness, the astonishing light of your own being." For many of us, self-judgment (that incessant voice of the Wicked Witch) is the biggest obstacle to our being kind to ourselves. Judging is easy — so easy that you may not even notice when you do it. When we judge something, we exclude other possibilities. If we judge a situation to be bad, we lose the opportunity to notice anything good about it. When we judge ourselves too harshly, we negate our better qualities.

Withdrawing judgment and replacing it with curiosity is a critical way to practice self-kindness. By learning to hold space for new information, to be inquisitive, we can quiet that limiting voice and reorient ourselves in the direction of new possibilities. We can transform our black-and-white thinking by asking ourselves two very important questions. (For this exercise, get a pen and a piece of paper, or open a Notes app on your smartphone, so you can write down your answers.)

First Ask Yourself . . .

1. What Am I Feeling?

When you go to the doctor, often she will ask what you're feeling. Do you have a backache? Chills? Have you been sneezing? She can then run some tests and figure out if your symptoms indicate the common cold or a more serious case of the flu. When we ask ourselves how we're feeling, we're doing something similar: checking up on our *emotional* health and well-being. Feelings are the symptoms of our being alive, and often what we're feeling can help us identify what we need.

Maybe you're feeling excited, sad, angry, disappointed, or fearful. Maybe you're thrilled about an upcoming vacation. Maybe you're sad because your teenage son has started to pull away from you and you miss the closeness you two once shared. Or maybe you feel depleted because your life lacks passion, purpose, or spontaneity. It might be difficult for you to pinpoint a specific emotion, and if that's the case, shift your attention to the body. Do you feel energetic? Perhaps you're experiencing pain in your lower back, or tightness in your shoulders. Observe whatever it is that stands out in the moment, and jot it down. Remember, don't pass judgment on your judgments. If you've ever tried meditating, you've probably heard that you should gently allow your thoughts to form and change like clouds in the sky. Your goal here is similar, but eventually, you want to be able to pick out which cloud is the biggest, which stands out the most *to you.*

Follow that cloud wherever it goes. Just as with noticing the voices inside your head clamoring to be heard, you're looking here to honor your feelings by acknowledging what they're trying to tell you.

2. What Do I Need Right Now?

We become self-critical when we feel we're lacking something in our lives. If we aren't getting what we need, support from a partner, for example, we may feel unappreciated and ignored, which in turn can make us feel angry, hostile, or depressed. Often these emotions trick us into thinking we're not good enough in the other person's eyes, not worthy enough of their attention or care. When we don't feel honored and respected, we can lose our footing and begin sliding down the slippery slope of self-judgment. Self-judgment is often a signal that something isn't right.

Now ask yourself — and jot down your answer in the same place you answered the question about feelings — what you think you need based on what you're feeling. When a doctor asks us what's wrong, she listens to our answer, evaluates, and then prescribes some sort of protocol to address what's bothering us. Your job is the same here. Now that you know what you're feeling, ask yourself what you *need.*

Once you have an idea of what you need, the radically kind thing to do for yourself is to act on that need. Maybe you notice you're feeling restless and anxious. You can *act* on that feeling by moving around to get out some of that pent-up energy; perhaps go for a walk or take a yoga class. This action makes you *feel* better by allowing you to be more centered, calmer.

If you feel sad and lonely, you can

act by scheduling a date night with your spouse, or call up those friends who always make you laugh. This act of kindness to yourself makes you feel happier, less lonely, by allowing you to be more emotionally connected with others.

Maybe you notice yourself feeling angry, or overly critical. You can act on this feeling by taking a pause to re-center yourself, perhaps with a cup of tea and some quiet time, which can make you feel more relaxed and joyful.

None of these actions has to be dramatic. Sometimes all you need is a few more hours of sleep, for the kids to clean up after themselves, some recognition from your coworkers, or to play fetch with your dog. Whatever it is, follow this longing to act. Acting on your own behalf is a powerful practice, and science has proven many times over how integral it is not just to you but to everyone around you.

Guilt: A Barrier to Self-Kindness

A whole book could be written on guilt and how it can upend lives. Many people, especially those who spend their days taking care of others, whether at home or at work, tend to feel guilty making time for themselves. When I went back to work after my first daughter was born, I felt so guilty that I withheld kindness from myself. With so many mixed feelings inside me —

longing to be with my daughter but also happy to be back to work — I needed to spend time talking to someone about these conflicting emotions. But I refused to go out to lunch or dinner with friends or even on a date night with my husband. I felt that taking time for myself meant stealing time from my daughter. Of course, that was not productive, and I certainly wasn't being kind to myself. It took some time for me to figure out that by being kind to myself, I could be a better mother, not the stressed-out, distracted mom who felt guilty all the time.

The Health Benefits of Self-Care

There are many reasons to be kind to yourself. It will help you feel calmer, more joyful; it will improve your health and give you the energy and will to extend that kindness to others. The most essential underlying reason to be kind to yourself, though, is that you are *worthy* of kindness, of self-care. I love the sound of the word *self-care.* It's as pleasant as the sounds in "spa weekend," "long bubble bath," "evening in with a good book," or "yoga retreat in Bali." But self-care is so much more than any of these. Sure, a few days meditating on a tropical island might be awesome, but it isn't necessary. What *is* necessary is that you do something kind for yourself.

The essence of self-care is addressing your own needs, managing your stress, pursuing your passions, feeling human connection, and taking a few minutes every so often simply to *be* with yourself, doing absolutely nothing beyond gathering your thoughts and breathing. Self-care is anything that makes you stronger and more resilient. That might be getting some exercise or eating high-quality food; meditating regularly or practicing that hobby that fulfills you; spending more time with supportive friends or just going for a morning walk.

What constitutes self-care for you

will be different from what constitutes self-care for someone else because it is about what *you* need in order to feel more capable of managing *your* life. Only you know what will increase your personal resilience. No matter what form your self-care takes, though, a significant body of research suggests that self-care is essential for basic health and functioning. One study showed that more social engagement, more positive self-talk, and better anger management were positively correlated with cardiac health,* while another showed that

* Fay C. M. Geisler et al., "Cardiac Vagal Tone Is Associated with Social Engagement and Self-Regulation," *Biological Psychology* 93, no. 2 (2013): 279–86.

self-care can reverse the toll stress takes on the immune system.* Regularly and deliberately addressing our physical, emotional, mental, and spiritual needs — in other words, being kind to ourselves — can improve our mood, reduce anxiety, foster healthy relationships, strengthen our immune system, and improve our self-concept.

THE NEGATIVE EFFECTS OF PUTTING YOURSELF LAST

One more reason to prioritize self-care is what can happen when you

* Thaddeus W. W. Pace et al., "Effect of Compassion Meditation on Neuroendocrine, Innate Immune, and Behavioral Responses to Psychosocial Stress," *Psychoneuroendocrinology* 34, no. 1 (2009): 87–98.

don't. Dr. Tasneem "Taz" Bhatia, who specializes in integrative medicine and women's health, contends that self-care is at the very core of living an energetic, healthy, and balanced life. In a recent conversation, she said, "When you look at the majority of health issues today, they're rooted in the lack of self-care. They're rooted in stress. You can rattle off twenty different diseases, and most of them go back to this."

The American Psychological Association would concur with Dr. Taz that self-care is not just a luxury but an imperative. Without it, people are more likely to suffer from distress, burnout, vicarious trauma from those they try to help (otherwise known as "compassion fatigue"), and impaired professional competence. People who do not care for themselves can become emotionally exhausted and feel less accomplished, less important. Their physical and emotional resources become depleted. They are more likely to develop addictive or compulsive behaviors, sleep problems, depression, and anxiety, and less likely to address the issues that normally come up in life.

Practicing kindness toward others is a form of self-care in that it has tangible physical and mental benefits for ourselves. According to the Mayo Clinic, volunteering your time to help other people without expectation of reward or return can lower stress hormones, boost self-confidence, decrease the risk of depression, provide a sense of purpose, help you stay physically and mentally active, and help forge social relationships; it also may even increase your life span.*

What's most interesting about all these findings is that we may know we need to take care of ourselves, but many of us don't act on it. Why not? A theory by psychotherapist Stefan Deutsch suggests that the reason is founded in a lack of self-

* "Helping People, Changing Lives: The 6 Health Benefits of Volunteering," *Speaking of Health* online newsletter, Mayo Clinic Health System, May 18, 2017, https://mayoclinichealthsystem.org/hometown-health/speaking-of-health/helping-people-changing-lives-the-6-health-benefits-of-volunteering.

love. Deutsch has written that "the self-love needed for self-care [is] missing. Academicians use terms like self-esteem, self-worth, self-support, self-care, but rarely self-love. That is left to the spiritual community. People don't realize that taking care of their own needs; eating, drinking, brushing their teeth, showering, wearing clean clothes, going to work are all acts of self-love." He argues that when people make excuses about not taking care of themselves, it is just another way of saying that they put themselves last on their list of priorities. Yet self-love is necessary for a functional and successful life — Deutsch calls it "literal nourishment" and says that loving yourself is as justifiable as eating and drinking.

And Dr. Taz advises, "Once you are kind to yourself, that's where you gain your power. Instead of having the energy to perhaps do just one thing, you have the energy and passion and creativity to do something bigger."

SELF-CARE 101

So, there is my prescription: self-care. Begin to love yourself enough to value your needs, and care for yourself in a way that will open the door for you to direct your kindness outward. The strength you derive from self-care will carry you through the challenges and stresses of life, so that you have the strength, health, and confidence to reach out to others with deep and sincere kindness. It can be challenging to make time for self-care, especially if you aren't in the habit of it, but here are ways to get started:

- *Carve out at least one hour a week for yourself.* Do something that you love and that feeds your soul. The time you set aside for this should be nonnegotiable, as important as a mandatory work meeting or paying your electric bill. Follow through, and don't compromise by giving this time away to others. Even if you bring others along on an out-ing, a spa day, or just a long morning of cozying up at home with a good book or a movie marathon, this time must be about you.

- *Forgive yourself.* Open your mind to the idea of forgiving yourself for something you did that you still feel guilty about. Forgiveness is a process. It can take years sometimes to get to a place where you let go of guilt or hard feelings. But a great first step is to tell yourself that you did the best you could at the time, with the information you had and the emotional place you were when it happened. We all make mistakes. What matters most is what we do afterward. What did you learn? How can you make it okay for yourself today?

- *Go to the doctor.* Get that annual physical. If you don't feel well, make an appointment and talk to a doctor. If you are experiencing anxiety or depression, see a counselor or therapist who can help you work through it. Stop ignoring your health issues because you don't think they're important or you don't want to know what they are. Your health, both physical and mental, is your most precious resource.

You don't have to wait for someone else to be kind to you. Kindness is a gift you can, and must, give yourself. Choose your self-care to fit what you need, not what anyone else needs, and make it a priority because you matter to the people who love you, and they want you to be happy, healthy, and calm. But maybe even more important, *you* matter to you. When you start living from the heart, you can find compassion for yourself, forgiveness for yourself, and a gentler attitude toward yourself and your circumstances. You can learn to love yourself better, in all the ways you need. Then and only then will you be able to love others fully.

5
Persona or Person?

Finding Your Authentic Self

Do you ever look in the mirror and ask yourself, "Who am I?" Some of us may answer: a wife, a mother, an accountant, an artist. But as we discussed earlier, we all contain a multitude of voices, each with particular opinions, needs, wants, insecurities, and doubts. With so many aspects of ourselves vying for our attention, answering the question "Who am I?" isn't always so simple. It requires going beyond what we do, what our roles in life are — beyond our appearance, our words, our actions — and opening a line of communication with our heart and emotions. And when we shift our attention to our emotions, it's easier to be kinder and gentler with ourselves because we see our true, honest, vulnerable, beautiful self staring back at us.

As you continue to practice seeing yourself with your heart, you will realize that much of the way you perceive the world and the people in it is a product of your long-standing self-concept. But all the past hurts and triumphs, and the stories you tell yourself about who you are, are your *persona,* not the intrinsic *you.* You may be a mother, but you are more than your children. You may be a comedian, but you are more than just a funny person. You may be an artist, but you are more than a writer, painter, or musician. Your persona is your public face. It doesn't define who you are inside, the essential *you* within yourself that has always been there and will always be.

WHO ARE YOU, *REALLY*?

Our personas, as interesting as they are, can sometimes confuse us and prevent us from seeing ourselves for who we really are. Without spending some time with yourself on yourself — in other words, taking time for reflection — you cannot hope to know yourself. And until you know yourself, you won't know whom you're being kind to when you practice self-kindness.

Deepak Chopra, renowned author, speaker, and spiritual adviser to millions, suggests practicing kindness toward oneself as a way of tapping into one's own authenticity. As he once told me:

> Self-directed kindness means getting to know your innermost being, which is beyond your ego identity. Often, we confuse our true self with our self-image, which is a social construct based on approval, disapproval, and public opinion. Your self-image is not yourself . . . When people

actually get in touch with their innermost being, they have total self-acceptance. They feel creative. They feel the freedom to choose their responses to the world. If your self-image is your provisional identity, your self is your core being, and your core being is automatically kind to itself and to others.

In other words, when you truly know your authentic self, you can't help but treat yourself with kindness and respect.

Of course, we often get in our own way. It's easy to confuse self-image with your true inner self and forget that the face you put on for the world does not always reflect your most essential self. This happens when you believe the "boxes" others put you in — "Diva!" "Not creative!" "Awkward!" "Not smart!" — as opposed to what you know deep inside to be true of yourself. The ego, that part of you that you project to the world, is easy to confuse with your innermost self, who you are without the influence of public opinion, expectations, or labels.

As we all know, it's easy to keep the real "you" covered up. Most of us don't like feeling vulnerable and exposed even with the people we love. There's a lot to say about vulnerability, and we'll get to it in the next chapter. For now, though, Dr. Brené Brown, research professor at the University of Houston Graduate College of Social Work and bestselling author, provides quite a bit of insight into the "emotional risk" many of us feel in our day-to-day lives. In an interview in *Forbes* magazine, Dr. Brown said, "Vulnerability is about showing up and being seen. It's tough to do that when we're terrified about what people might see or think. When we're fueled by the fear of what other people think or that gremlin that's constantly whispering 'You're not good enough' in our ear, it's tough to show up. We end up hustling for our worthiness."*

* Dan Schawbel interview with Brené Brown, "Brené Brown, How Vulnerability Can Make Our Lives Better," *Forbes* online, April 21,

In the end, we add layer upon layer of protection, until we forget exactly who we were before we needed all that protection.

Yet, our innermost being, our real self, is a prize worth searching for. As Deepak Chopra contends, the innermost being is capable of things the ego or self-image can't achieve. Your innermost being is completely self-accepting. It is creative. It is free. It can act however it needs to act, without the influence of public opinion. It is incapable of judging itself, and it is automatically kind.

2013, https://www.forbes.com/sites/danschawbel/2013/04/21/brene-brown-how-vulnerability-can-make-our-lives-better/#474c823336c7.

But how do you tap into your innermost being? As Dr. Brown says, by daring greatly, by "owning our vulnerability and understanding it as the birthplace of courage and the other meaning-making experiences in our lives." Sometimes that courage can be as basic as performing a simple act of kindness toward ourselves, by doing something that makes us happy.

According to happiness expert Barbara Fredrickson, a psychology professor at the University of North Carolina, positive actions and emotions broaden our sense of possibilities, open our minds, and allow us to build valuable new skills. Whereas negative emotions narrow mind-sets and spark the urge to attack or flee, positive emotions spark the urge to play and explore the world and ourselves; they enhance creativity. And where negative emotions (stress, fear, and insecurity) are more likely to encourage us to build up those protective layers around ourselves, to protect us from danger and bad feelings, a positive, playful, exploratory mindset is just what we need to see our innermost selves more clearly. Of course, doing things that make us happy does not make us inherently kinder, but if we approach our search for happiness with warmth and respect for ourselves and others, we'll find that kindness and joy are closely related.

Child's Play and Your Authentic Self

One of the best ways I've found to spark positive emotions and help reclaim our essential selves is to play. Doing what you loved to do as a child can connect you immediately and viscerally with your authentic self. It's no surprise that in recent years, millions and millions of adult coloring books have been sold around the world. Not only is coloring a fine meditative practice, but it returns us to an earlier, seemingly simpler time in our lives, when playing with a box of crayons and a coloring book was enough to make us so very happy. Being kind to ourselves sometimes means revisiting those things we once loved but may have lost, bringing them back into our lives.

You can let yourself play *now.* If you once loved to paint, then buy some paints and a few canvases, or sign up for a painting class. Did you like to bowl? Get some friends together and go bowling. You can bake cookies or take a child to a playground and swing on a swing. You can reread a book you loved as a kid; most of the classics are still in print. If you felt free and alive as a child in dance class, you could take a class now; there are many classes for adult beginners. You can even just lie on the grass under a tree on a sunny day and look for shapes in the clouds. Nobody is telling you that you can't do this, so why not try?

While these are fun activities, play is not just about having fun. It's also a way to get back to the basics, to remind yourself that before you accumulated all your responsibilities, you loved just *being.* Plain and simple, you loved to be alive.

Of course, the world is a serious place, and we should take it seriously, but the joy of play is a kindness most of us can afford to give ourselves, a gift that can lighten our spirits and reorder our priorities, inching us ever closer to the essential people we are, that inner self we see only with the heart.

6
"Can You Help Me?"

Receiving in Order to Give

As we touched on in the last chapter, one of the most challenging ways to be kind to yourself is to be vulnerable in front of other people. This sounds counterintuitive, but hear me out: being vulnerable can feel uncomfortable, and may not seem like a kindness toward yourself, but when you admit your weaknesses and share your essential self with others, you allow them to step in and meet you with kindness.

Vulnerability, then, is not only the bedrock of intimacy and meaningful relationships, but also a way of inviting goodwill into our lives.

When you are vulnerable, you are unguarded, open, and trusting of others. You let your true self out for the world to see. Being vulnerable is difficult because it means surrendering control. Your heart is on your sleeve. Your mind is spoken. Your soul is bared.

Four Magic Words

The fastest, easiest way of being vulnerable with others is to acknowledge that you need help. In fact, "Can you help me" are the four magic words for both receiving and giving kindness. When we ask for help, we are admitting that we might not be strong enough physically, mentally, or emotionally to handle a task or situation on our own. Conceding that you need someone else is humbling and can make you feel vulnerable. We all want to think we know it all or can handle whatever comes our way. But when we drop such pretenses, we realize that our asking for help is really a gift to others because it allows them a chance to be kind to us. Asking for help usually lowers everyone's guard. It gives someone else an opportunity to do a good deed. According to bestselling author Gretchen Rubin, most people are happier when asked for a small favor because "providing support is just as important as getting support. By offering people a way to provide support, you generate good feelings in them."*

Of course, it is usually easier to ask for physical help than emotional help. Asking a stranger to hold the elevator for us or a neighbor to watch our dog for the weekend is one thing. Asking a friend for emotional support because your kids have been sick all week, you haven't slept, you're having problems at work, and you feel at the end of your rope — well, that's

* Gretchen Rubin, "To Make a Friend, Ask Someone for a Favor," September 3, 2010, https://gretchenrubin.com/2010/09/if-you-want-to-make-a-friend-let-someone-do-you-a-favor/.

another thing entirely. Many times, we don't want to burden another person with our problems or project the impression that we aren't strong enough to deal with them on our own.

Yet, nobody can manage all their problems on their own; we aren't wired that way. We can't do everything all the time, and in fact, human beings are made to rely on one another for help. If you're trying to figure out a problem in your own heart — whether it's with your partner, your child, your parents, or a sibling; or whether it's a work situation, a health situation, a big decision, or even a spiritual dilemma or crisis — you can say to someone you love and trust, "I can't figure this out. Can you help me talk it through?"

The Gift of Professional Help

What if you're married to someone who is bipolar and you need help? What if your son is sinking into a major depression and you're out of your mind with sadness and worry? What if you're lonely in your marriage, but religious convictions limit your choices? When life throws a challenge your way that is too difficult to manage on your own or with the help of friends, professional help can be a lifesaver. Many people balk at going to a counselor or therapist for various reasons: fear, lack of time, or just not wanting to admit we can't handle a problem or a crisis on our own, to name a few. But these professionals are perfectly positioned to say yes when you ask for help. They can support you in ways that even your closest friend or your partner cannot. Being vulnerable enough to make that call is a gift to yourself, and to those who love you and know you're struggling. When your car breaks down, do you fault your car for being weak? Do you shame your car? Of course not. You call a mechanic. The same applies to emotional distress. If your problem is too big for a friend to handle, call a professional, or use local or online support groups for people going through a similar situation, for more targeted help.

THE GIFT OF VULNERABILITY

If you're still thinking that asking for help is selfish, think again. Even asking for simple physical help is a gift to others as well as to yourself. As someone with a background in child psychology and who has worked in children's television for almost thirty years, I've done the research, especially in developmental theory, and the research shows that asking others for help is motivating and empowering for them as well as for you. Human beings want to be useful. When we help, we feel empowered, our self-worth skyrockets, and our bonds with other people become stronger.

I used this idea on the very first episode of *Blue's Clues,* a popular live-action/animated educational children's television series on Nick-elodeon starring a puppy named Blue. We wanted to reach out and give the kids at home an opportu-nity to "help," to be an active part of our world. In the episode, "Steve," an adult, needs the help of preschoolers to figure out what Blue wants for a snack. Steve leans in close to the camera, makes eye contact with the children watching, and asks them, "Can you help me?" The first time he did this, it was as if he had said, "Abracadabra!" Those four words were magic. Kids jumped up, pointed to clues, and talked back to Steve. And in every episode thereafter, we used those four magic words.

Your own "Can you help me?" can take many forms, from the dramatic to the mundane, but the better you get at asking for help when you genuinely need it (and not when you're just feeling lazy), the more often you'll receive the gift of human kindness and support for your own needs, and the more often you'll give others the opportunity to practice kindness on you.

When you get comfortable with "Can you help me?" you can progress to a more advanced level of vulnerability: of purposefully allowing yourself to be heart-seen. Your relationships depend upon it. Dr. Brené Brown often says in her talks that being vulnerable means being "your true self." In other words, vulnerability is heart-seeing ourselves and allowing our true selves to be seen by others. Give that inner you some fresh air and sunshine. Be that person on the outside, not just on the inside.

To be vulnerable is a great act of courage. It takes strength to share ourselves with others. There are fewer things harder, and there are fewer things more beautiful. When you can access your humility, soften your exterior, and open the window to your soul to let someone else come in, yes, you will feel vulnerable and exposed, but you will also be seeable — and that is the only way a relationship can ever be deeply meaningful and reciprocal. Having profound emotional bonds with other people is one of the most rewarding aspects of life, and vulnerability is the key to creating those bonds.

III
Be Kind to Others

7
Hit the Pause Button

Seeing Others with Your Heart

In many ways, reaching out to others with kindness is easier than being kind to yourself. It certainly sounds more virtuous. For example, most people feel they should guide a tourist who's lost his way, volunteer at a soup kitchen once a month, or help a friend move to a new apartment.

Knowing how to reach out to others requires taking the same initial step you took when learning how to be kind to yourself: heart-seeing. We can celebrate acts of generosity for what they are, kindness in action, but truly embracing radical kindness means moving past the knowledge that we "should" be kind to others and actually seeing within others what they really need. This gives us the information we require to live our lives with kindness as the foundation for all we do.

Sometimes it's easy to see others with kindness, especially those who are kind to us — those we love, those with agreeable temperaments, cute children, strangers who smile and reach out. It's easier to heart-see and act lovingly toward someone who is cuddly or cute or generous than it is to heart-see someone who is snarly or argumentative or irritable.

CHANNEL MISTER SNUFFLEUPAGUS

When I was a kid, I loved *Sesame Street*'s Bert and Ernie. They were great role models for how to be a friend. But when it came to kindness, nobody beat Mister Snuffleupagus, the woolly mammoth–like creature with love in his heart for everyone. Puppeteer and performer Martin Robinson, the man who gives voice to "Snuffy," described the delightful pachyderm's personality in simple terms: "Snuffy can only see kindness. When Oscar the

Grouch is complaining, for example, Snuffy does not perceive it as negative. He thinks Oscar is hilarious." In other words, rather than responding to Oscar's negativity with frustration, Snuffy looks for the best in him — or at least sees that he has feelings, too. That is the essence of heart-seeing: seeing past bad behavior to the real-life human who, like many of us, is imperfect in articulating his emotions.

Like Snuffy, we can choose to look deeper, past another person's grouchiness, irritability, snarky comments, gossip, impatience, and all those things good people exhibit when they're having a bad day. Remaining calm and compassionate in the face of negativity can take the wind out of the sails of anyone's anger and irritation. More important, seeing the good in someone who is not acting "good" hones our kindness skills. It asks the most from us. It demands the most persistent heart-seeing. It demands looking without assumptions. It demands a dramatic check on what may be our first impulse: to meet bad behavior with more bad behavior.

The Power of the Pause Button

In the face of negativity, we all make assumptions based on appearance and behavior — about people we know but especially about people we don't know. The secret to avoiding this is what I call "the pause." When you hit the Pause button, you are giving yourself time to recover, time to process. The pause is one of the smartest, most effective tools you can use in a challenging situation. Pausing prevents preprogrammed reactions. Plutarch once observed, "Silence at the proper season is wisdom, and better than any speech," and we can use this observation as a strategy for helping ourselves help others.

With any potentially negative interaction, use the Pause button. Before you speak or act, stop, be quiet, and ask yourself, "What does this person need?" Then ask yourself, "How can I help?" Sometimes we get so wrapped up in what we think, feel, or believe that we don't realize we're not *seeing.* We're assuming. That can lead to unkind words and actions.

Consider a mother who, after a hard day at work, snaps at her daughter for not picking up her toys. This mother doesn't intend to be mean. She may be feeling frustrated because she's told her daughter countless times to clean up after herself, and she may not be seeing this one instance as unique. She may not be looking for what is really going on. It is likely that the daughter's seeming disobedience can be attributed to something else: perhaps she's had a difficult day at school and needs someone to listen before she can muster the energy to pick up her room.

By catching yourself, pausing, and taking a breath before responding, you also give yourself the opportunity to hit the Reset button on the situation, turning what could become an unkind reaction into a kind one. By hitting Pause and asking yourself, "What does this person need?" and "How can I help?" you're able to choose the best course of action, rather than the first course of action that occurs to you. In short, hitting Pause rewires your brain not to react reflexively. It may not seem easy, especially if you're hot-headed by nature, but pausing to check your kindness level will change for the better how you respond to people and how they respond to you.

The pause is an opportunity to reflect, especially during moments of tension, so that you can pivot toward kindness and compassion rather than criticism. The pause helps you see a difficult situation through more empathetic eyes, rather than dismissing it or defaulting to a hurried exit.

So, when you're tempted to make a snap judgment . . . pause.

When you're tempted to say something angry . . . pause.

When you're tempted to lecture, shame, or argue . . . pause.

When you pause, you allow yourself to see and understand someone else's point of view, even when it doesn't agree with yours. It means waiting, watching, and seeing, rather than reacting with anger, fear, or irritation. For instance, if somebody cuts you off in traffic or pushes in front of you to pass through a doorway, your first thought is probably not a kind one. But if you pause and look with your heart, you're able to give this person the benefit of the doubt. If you can shift your thinking from "That guy cut me off!" to "I hope that guy is okay," you have avoided a chain reaction of anger and defensiveness in favor of feelings of compassion and forgiveness. You have also changed your response from being about you to being about the other person. By valuing that other person's experience alongside your own, you begin to heart-see.

Heart-seeing — that is, assuming the best about other people — can become a guiding force in your day-to-day life. You can respond to your kids in a kinder, gentler way when they are having a hard time at school. You can find something in your personal experience to inspire and comfort a friend despairing of ever finding his soul mate. You can suggest a good book or a qualified therapist to someone crumpling under the burden of caring for a child newly diagnosed with an illness.

SEE THE INNER CHILD IN OTHERS

Even before you do a kindness for others, try to feel the kindness first. Imagine the good feelings that come from treating others with heightened levels of respect and generosity. It's not easy, but there are ways to make it easier.

One foolproof strategy is to imagine everyone you meet as the person they were at four years old. (This should be easy to do because part of being radically kind is being hyperaware of your own inner child.) After all, we're all the children of *someone.* Say to yourself, "This is somebody's son, somebody's daughter."

Remember that all of us are on a

similar journey through life. Almost everyone wants to love and be loved. Seeing other people as children can help neutralize any bad feelings you have toward them. You will be aware of your shared humanity, and feel a genuine sense of camaraderie, of "We're all in this together." By imagining others as children, you begin to see everyone as a pure, vulnerable soul, someone who, like you, is just trying to figure out where they fit in a world that's often spinning too fast to care.

8
Kindness to Family and Friends

Heart-Seeing Your Inner Circle

While kindness to ourselves is of great importance, it is essential to realize that a radically kind life is a life of community. We truly experience the depth and power of authentic kindness only by living, working, celebrating, and mourning with others. Whether a community takes the form of a family, a circle of friends, or a group of colleagues, by the very nature of our human hearts, we are called to engage and connect with others.

Of course, interacting with others isn't always easy or fun. As philosopher Jean-Paul Sartre wrote in his play *No Exit,* "Hell is other people." But what he failed to mention is that heaven is other people, too. The loving relationships we forge with others make our lives worth living. So, we owe it to ourselves and to our loved ones to nurture those relationships with kindness. After all, each of us shares the same need for love and compassion, and the same need to be seen, listened to, honored, and cared for.

Sometimes it's easy to practice radical kindness toward others. But more often than not, it's challenging, especially when those we love the most push our buttons the hardest or have significant needs. Radical kindness can ask a lot from us. But by taking it one step at a time, we can all build toward stronger, more intimate, more caring relationships.

Step One: Notice

The first step (just as for being kind to ourselves) is to notice. What do those closest to you — your family members, your friends, and your work colleagues — need? Maybe your son needs extra attention from you because he broke up with his girlfriend. Maybe an elderly neighbor needs a ride to the doctor. Maybe your friend needs a night out after a difficult week at work. Whoever they are, pay attention to the people around you. They might not even know they're suffering. Many people don't voice their needs and desires as much as they should, so the onus is on us to pay attention to others' body language or verbal clues, such as the evidence of exhaustion we hear in our father's voice or that expression on your best friend's face that shows she's feeling down. Don't assume you know what the people you love are feeling. Heart-see them without prejudgment. You may be surprised at what you find.

Step Two: Extend Kindness

The second step entails acting upon what you see by extending kindness to the people in your circle. Radical kindness has no more appropriate place than in our most valued connections. If you take for granted the people you love, assume that they know how you feel or that you know how they feel, or don't give them all they need because you tell yourself you can always do it later — they'll always be there, right? — it may be time to refresh your ideas about kindness. We all want to be the parent who pauses to listen; the adult child who steps off her busy, spinning world to visit her aging parents; the sibling who lends a hand;

the partner, spouse, or friend who shows love through actions. The people you love the most are the ones who can most directly benefit from the kindness you radiate. As you set a new standard for your personal relationships, one in which you act first and foremost from a place of warmth, caring, and heart-seeing, the kindness you give will be returned to you.

FIFTEEN MINUTES OF KINDNESS

In his book *MicroShifts* and on his website, author Gary Jansen writes that even though we might all be different from one another in terms of who we are, where we come from, and what we possess, we have in common precisely 1,440 minutes in each day to live our lives.* Of course, how we use that time varies from one person to the next.

What I love is how Jansen challenges the reader to contemplate how life would change if we took just *fifteen minutes* every twenty-four hours (only about 1 percent of every day) and made a tiny switch in the way we looked at and did things. This radical "microshift" involves performing one small kind act for another person. The possibilities and the rewards are limitless. Imagine all the power in a small fifteen-minute shift.

* Gary Jansen, "What Would Happen If You Gave Just One Percent of Your Life to Changing the World?," http://www.garyjansen.com/.

What could you do in fifteen minutes that would radiate kindness?

- Turn off smartphones, computers, and the TV and spend time instead talking with your spouse and children.
- Plant flowers in your grandmother's garden.
- Read Dr. Seuss books or any of dozens of classic children's novels to your kids. (Imagine rediscovering great books such as *Anne of Green Gables, Black Beauty, Little Women, The Secret Garden,* or *King Arthur* with a little one!)
- Walk the dog for your elderly neighbor, or bring her garbage

bins in and out each week on trash pickup days.

- Spend fifteen minutes a day writing down memories you hold dear so that you can share them in later years with the people you love.

Every day, in every interaction with the people we love, we have an opportunity to open our hearts to them, give them our full attention, and strive to see what they really need. Each action is an acknowledgment and a celebration of those people who have helped us through life.

Your gestures of radical kindness could be small and yet still be radical. Sometimes just picking up your towel from the bathroom floor or loading the dishwasher can do the trick. They could be quiet, such as listening instead of talking, supporting instead of always being the one to seek support, or noticing what someone needs and doing it without having to be asked. Maybe your act of kindness could be simply giving your full attention to someone. There will always be time later to look at your smartphone, pay the bills, make that call, or clean the house. Stay present as much as you can in the now and offer those around you the gift of your undivided attention.

Looking back over a whole childhood full of people and television personalities, I realize that this is precisely what made Fred Rogers stand out. He had that remarkable ability to make every viewer feel as if he were speaking directly to them. He made me feel that I really was his friend. If you can still your racing thoughts enough to be absolutely and fully present with someone, then you, like Mister Rogers, can make that person feel that they are the *only* person in the room. They will feel that they are important, validated, heard. Why? Because when you give your full attention to someone, you are, in effect, communicating important messages: *You matter. You are more important than my to-do list. I am here for you. You can trust me.* When you learn to do this as a matter of course — that is, when it becomes your default way of connecting with the people closest to you — an amazing thing begins to happen. Kindness becomes contagious.

Kindness Is Contagious

Research has shown that acting kindly actually elevates the impulse for kinder behavior in others. That's right. Witnessing kindnesses performed by others elevates the impulse to perform kind acts oneself — what in one study researchers called "moral elevation." In a study published in *Biological Psychology,* researchers discovered that when participants watched scenarios of people suffering and then having that suffering relieved by a kind act, it had the unusual effect of activating both the sympathetic and parasympathetic nervous systems simultaneously, as well as the medial prefrontal cortex, which is the center for empathy and the ability to predict the thoughts and behavior of others.* The researchers theorized that when we witness kind acts, we first feel the stress from the suffering of others; then feel good and calm when we see the suffering relieved; and finally, are able to relate personally to what we've seen, which makes us more likely to feel the impulse of kind-

* W. T. Piper et al., "Autonomic and Prefrontal Events During Moral Elevation," *Biological Psychology* 108, no. 51 (2015): 5.

ness toward others.

Another study, by researchers at the University of California, Los Angeles, along with the University of Cambridge and the University of Plymouth in the United Kingdom, involved showing groups of people one of three videos: a humorous video, a nature documentary, or clips from *The Oprah Winfrey Show* demonstrating kindness. Afterward, the participants were asked to volunteer to help with another task. Those who had watched the *Oprah* clips were the most likely to volunteer.*

* Shannon Mehner, "Kindness Is Contagious, New Study Finds," *Helix,* April 21, 2010, https://helix.northwestern.edu/article/kindness-contagious-new-study-finds.

In a 2016 article in *Scientific American,* researcher Jamil Zaki related study results that demonstrate that "people imitate not only the particulars of positive actions, but also the spirit underlying them. This implies that kindness itself is contagious, and that it can cascade across people, taking on new forms along the way." In one study, Zaki and his researchers gave a group of people one dollar and showed them a list of charities, giving them the opportunity to donate some of the money or keep it. After donating, participants saw manipulated data showing either that many people had donated an average of 75 percent of their bonuses (showing a "generous world") or that most people had donated only 25 percent of the money (showing a "stingy world"). Those who witnessed the "generous" statistics became more likely to donate more of their money. Zaki and colleagues also performed a follow-up study, in which people who had observed others donating either generously or stingily had to complete a seemingly unrelated task: responding to a "pen pal" who had written a note describing the ups and downs of his life. Those participants who had witnessed the more generous donations wrote "friendlier, more empathetic, more supportive notes" than those who had witnessed the less generous donations. Zaki concluded that "kindness evolves as it diffuses, 'infecting' behaviors through which new individuals can express it."*

In short, when you are in proximity to people who behave a certain way, you are more likely to behave that way, too. For example, when you choose to radiate kindness to all those around you, that behavior is likely to rub off on others. This goes both ways, of course: families in the habit of snapping at one another perpetuate a climate of curt insensitivity, while families in the habit of being kind to one another perpetuate insight, healing,

* Jamil Zaki, "Kindness Contagion," *Scientific American,* July 26, 2016, https://www.scientificamerican.com/article/ kindness-contagion.

concern, and compassion.

You probably don't have to work too hard to imagine coming home tired and irritated after a long day — who among us has not? Imagine, though, that after a day like that, you come home to find your partner already at home making dinner, but the kitchen is a mess. You have a choice in that moment. You could say something like "Oh, great, look at this mess. I suppose I'll have to clean it up — and after the day I've had!" likely prompting your partner to snap back, "At least somebody is around to cook dinner!" Or, you could hit Pause and choose kindness. You could say something like "What a long day. Thank you for taking care of dinner. That means a lot to me. I don't think I could have managed it on a day like this." This type of reaction prompts a different type of a response. Your partner, more likely to be sympathetic to the fact that you're feeling depleted, may inquire about your day and really listen from the heart (and may even end up cleaning up the messy kitchen so you don't have to). In other words, you have the choice: to brew up an argument or to initiate a meaningful conversation that leads to authentic connection.

This contagious kindness can influence your family dynamic in the best ways. It will model kindness and teach your kids by example to be kinder in their interactions with their siblings, their friends, and you. It will show your parents that you love them, even if you've had your troubles in the past. That can be a great kindness to parents who feel guilt over past misunderstandings or wrongdoings and who desire forgiveness from their adult children. It can deepen your relationship with your partner, fostering more intimacy and a stronger bond. It can improve your friendships, making them more meaningful and more mutually supportive.

THE POWER OF GRATITUDE

As with everything in life, especially during times of stress and strain, when things get out of whack, you're going to have to practice new responses, and one of the most potent is gratitude — another powerful "baby step" toward mastering kindness with the people you know well and love. Thanking a loved one for making dinner is just one example. The goal of radical kindness is to let others know they matter, and what better way than to express gratitude for what that other person does in the world? What better way to make them feel seen, appreciated, valued, and loved? As you move through your day, look for opportunities to express gratitude openly and freely with the people in your life:

Thank you for taking that meeting.

Thank you for loaning me your umbrella.

Thank you for watching the kids while I ran to the store.

Thank you for always being so optimistic. It helps the whole family to look on the bright side.

You can also learn to express kindness better just by showing that you're present with someone else, that you *see them.* Mastering old patterns of reactivity will necessitate some hard work on your part, especially when the habits of family members or friends are deeply ingrained. But again, you can always break a bad habit. Either privately or with the help of a partner, practice new ways of responding to the kinds of situations that typically trip you up at work and home. Some examples might be:

You look upset. Are you all right? Do you want to talk about it?

How have you been doing? We haven't talked in a while, and I miss you.

Let me get that for you. I want to help.

You deserve this. You've worked so hard.

How is it going with that trouble at school?

What can I do for you right now that would make your day easier?

In case I haven't told you in a while, I love you.

Of course, the importance of these interactions lies not exclusively in the words spoken, but also in the sincerity behind them, and the actions that follow.

THE POWER OF "HOW CAN I HELP?"

On my PBS Kids show *Daniel Tiger's Neighborhood,* we teach preschoolers that when something goes wrong, they should say not just "I'm sorry" but "I'm sorry. How can I help?" This is a great tip for dealing with people of all ages. Follow up every apology or query with "How can I help?" which I think of as the externally directed version of "Can you help me?" Adding "How can I help?" will prompt you to act when you see someone in need at any level. "I'm sorry" (empathy) + "How can I help?" (action) is the important equation for making sure your kindness practice leads to radical change.

Whether they realize it or not, all humans seek connection. If connection is what matters most, then why do anything other than nurture it with kindness? That old saying is true: Nobody on their deathbed says, "I wish I'd spent more time at the office." People most often say that they wish they had experienced more, been less afraid to be themselves, and most of all, prioritized people over work and possessions. At the end of your life, the people whom you love are what will matter most to you, and you can let them know it today.

SETTING YOUR INTENTION 101

How does the practice of radical kindness change in the instance of unhappy relationships? Misunderstandings, arguments, and jealousy are facts of life. When you experience them, friendships you thought were rock-solid can suddenly mess up your mind, preventing you from getting a good night's sleep or concentrating at work. What then? How do you lead with kindness when you're feeling hurt, betrayed, angry, or abandoned?

Dr. Wayne Dyer suggests using the power of intention. Similar to how athletes, musicians, and test-takers practice visualizing success, setting an intention involves directing your choices and actions toward a desired outcome. Setting your intention is about establishing a starting point of genuine compassion, acting upon it, and, finally, trusting that kindness will somehow win in the end.

Here's a simple visualization exercise called the Pink Bubble. This technique was popularized by author and speaker Shakti Gawain. Over the years, I've combined this practice with something called "loving-kindness meditation," which many Buddhists use to send love and kindness to friends, family, strangers, and even the world. I find that this exercise is valuable, not only for sending love to those who are easy to love, but especially for resetting a negative mental framework surrounding a situation you are struggling with. Feelings of hurt, anger, betrayal, or an inability to forgive can all begin to heal with the regular practice of this meditation. I believe it is powerful because even though bad things happen sometimes, and people sometimes hurt you, how you think about what happened is the most influential aspect of being kind to yourself and others, and even helps you to find the will as well as the compassion to forgive. It sounds simple, but give it a try to experience its power. Here is how you do it:

- Begin by briefly acknowledging the conflict, misunderstanding, ill will, worry, stress, aggravation, or situation you are seeking to reframe — or the person who is the subject of it (whether you are angry with them or worried about them or just feel they need extra love).

- Relax your mind and visualize a happy and joyful scene in your life. In your mind, turn that scene into your own "movie"; or perhaps focus on a happy memory from childhood — something that has a kind and peaceful resolution.
- Repeat these words to yourself: "I send love and kindness to . . ." then name the person, the situation, the event, or whatever it is that you are

working on.

- Imagine a pink glistening bubble surrounding the person or the situation, conflict, or event.
- In your mind, allow the bubble to float away from you, no longer within reach, carrying the object of your focus with it. The bubble symbolizes the intention you've set to put a new frame around this person or problem — a frame of love and kindness rather than whatever you were feeling before (worry, anger, and so on). As the pink bubble floats away, recognize that you can now give up any sense of control you thought you had regarding

the outcome of the situation. You have surrounded the person or situation with love; then let it go. This is not giving up — it is a way to set your mind free from the trap it has created for itself, and to reset your feelings about the person or situation.

Perhaps this exercise seems metaphysical or even a bit impractical to you, compared with taking some sort of concrete action. And yet, remember that how you act is usually a product of how you feel. This exercise will help you to transform your own feelings so that you can act with more compassion and understanding. It also gives you something productive to do, mentally, when the situation is not something you can physically do anything about. It shifts your focus in a productive way.

Setting your intention is about visualizing genuine compassion, acting upon it, and, finally, trusting that kindness will win out in the end. Intention setting is the visualization of the hope and positivity that come from putting an image to your thoughts of kindness. When you see yourself and others with your own heart, you are sending love and kindness out to where it needs to go. You are then on the path toward radical kindness.

9
Lean In

The Art of Active Listening

Everyone — children, spouses, siblings, parents, friends — wants to be heard. Listening is the half of a conversation that is most often neglected, yet it is just as essential as making your point or expressing your emotions. It is also a vital tool in your kindness toolbox, a simple way to be kind to anyone, no matter how well you know them. Giving someone your full attention, concentrating on what they're saying, and meeting what they say with genuine curiosity and attentiveness is one of the greatest kindnesses you can perform for another person, and all it takes is making the time to be in the moment.

When the Answer Isn't "I'm Fine"

Have you ever bumped into a friend on the street? You smile and say, "Hi! How are you?" expecting their spontaneous answer of "Fine," so you can both continue on your way. But then your friend actually tells you how they are. A genuine answer to the question "How are you?" is not always quick, and it can sometimes even be emotional. The answer could be "I'm good, but my father just had surgery and I'm afraid he won't make it."

What do you do now? Do you check the time and scurry off? Or do you use this moment to lean in, lock eyes with your friend, and empathetically ask for more details. When we ask a question, we then need to be open to receive a real answer — and to listen to it actively.

Listening is not a passive act. Yes, it may seem that way; after all, the speaker is the one doing the talking. She's moving her mouth and, if she's like me, speaking with her hands! The listener is merely sitting there quietly. But listening is a lot harder than it looks, and if we're honest with ourselves, most of us will admit we're not always the best listeners. We might get distracted; we might be worrying about a deadline we need to meet, mentally scrolling through our to-do lists, or waiting for the other person to pause long enough so we can voice our own opinion. Though most of us usually have good intentions and even a real interest in the conversation, good intentions alone don't make us good listeners.

In "Listening to People," an article published in the *Harvard Business Review* way back in 1957, but still applicable today, authors Ralph G. Nichols and Leonard A. Stevens analyzed the primary problems people have with listening. We think faster than we speak. So, while we're listening to others, the authors write, our brains often begin to multitask, and we get distracted and can lose the thread. Instead, the authors suggest, we should be using that extra brain bandwidth to focus more fully on who is speaking, thinking critically about what the person is saying, showing our interest, asking questions, paraphrasing, drawing connections, and making sure we understand.

Giving someone your undivided attention is a sign of respect and appreciation. When you listen carefully to someone, you communicate that that person's feelings and opinions matter. Active listening provides the other person with a safe haven to express their vulnerability. When a friend, family member, colleague, or even a stranger opens up to us, they are giving us a gift of honesty, one that we should protect and cherish. They are sharing something of their inner lives with us, a piece of their authentic self. Too often we attend to conversation in a mindless way, and miss what the other person is saying. This devalues the other and, in turn, devalues us, because we are not being as kind as we could be. We are dismissing a show of vulnerability from another.

When the topic is not an emotional one or is seemingly unimportant, or when the person speaking tends to be chatty, it's not always easy for us to listen as fully as we should or to avoid judging what is being said before we have all the information. This is where practice makes perfect.

Active Listening 101

Try this method for active listening so you can comprehend better and give the gift of kindness by being fully present when someone else is speaking:

- Put down your smartphone and look fully away from your computer, the television, or any other screen. Filter out background distractions as best you can. Don't look over the person's shoulder or around the room to see what else is going on or what the source of other noises might be.

- Make eye contact with the person speaking. Literally lean toward them as they speak.
- Listen to their words. Think about their ideas. Concentrate!
- Do not interrupt — even when you vehemently disagree or if the speaker says something mistaken or untrue. You can always mention it later, when it's your turn to speak. Don't let it distract you.
- Pay attention to the speaker's expression, tone, mood, and body language.
- Ask clarifying questions and paraphrase. For instance, "Let

me stop you for a quick moment. So, your mother is still upset over what your boyfriend said at dinner, and you feel caught in the middle?" This not only helps you focus, but ensures that you're correctly hearing the person in front of you.

- If you start to think of a response while the person is still speaking, or of what you want to add to the conversation, stop yourself. You'll have plenty of time to respond later. Tune back in to the words you're hearing. Let yourself experience listening without any thought of speaking. Remember, this is not about you. It's about listening to someone else.

- When the person is done speaking, don't jump right in. Wait a moment. Maybe they have more to say. Not everyone is a fast talker.
- Resist adding your two cents until you're asked for it. Most of the time, people are not looking for solutions; they're looking to express themselves and have someone take them seriously.
- Finally, consider the speaker's point of view. You've been on his end of the conversation — as the one hoping the person you're speaking to is actively listening to *you.* Speaking to

an active listener *feels* much different from speaking to a distracted listener. You can't control whether someone else is actively listening, but you can control whether *you* are. And remember: kindness is contagious! When you listen actively, you open up a connection that says, in a classic Mister Rogers way, "It's you I like. Right here, right now. Go on, I'm here. I'm listening."

At some point, the other person may feel at ease and turn the subject back to you by asking you what you think. At this point, the other person is giving you permission to offer advice or share your perspective. In an unstated way, this person is asking for help. But again, this is about the other person. Keep your response short and sincere, and then allow the person to respond to you and continue speaking.

Active listening as a kindness can be truly transformative. Making a friend, family member, or colleague feel heard is a simple way to make them feel cared for. It can save marriages and strengthen the bond of any relationship. By actively listening, you're giving someone a gift of your presence, of your acceptance, of your kindness, and without the expectation of receiving anything in return — all from spending only a few minutes of your time.

Ultimately, the kindness involved in active listening isn't just heart-seeing, but heart-*listening,* that is, lovingly and patiently hearing what the people in our lives have to say and handling their thoughts with care. This way of engaging with others highlights the beauty of our shared humanity — the desire for friendship, peace, trust, patience, and understanding — and honors the simple need to be heard that we all share.

10
Beyond First Impressions

Seeing the Person Underneath

It's not easy to see someone deeply, with your heart, even when you know that person well. And it's even harder to heart-see a stranger — someone who will probably wonder why you're staring deeply into his eyes! You cannot hope to understand everything about someone if you have no personal experience or history with that person.

Even so, we are prone to forming

preconceived notions about people we don't know. Everyone has preconceptions. The trick is to recognize them as preconceptions, rather than mistaking them for indicators of truth. Preconceptions are generally based on first impressions, what we see on the surface — age, gender, appearance, posture, social status, financial status, educational status, athletic ability, intelligence, how someone talks, how they act. But this is only a one-dimensional view of a person.

If you rely on your preconceptions and prejudices, you might end up going down the wrong road, making false assumptions, or coming to incorrect conclusions about who someone is. This could unfairly color your entire future relationship with that person, for good or bad. What if you dismissed someone who could have become a close, valuable friend? What if you missed an opportunity to learn something new and interesting about the world? Or what if you jumped to hire a person who at first seemed right for a job, but who had underlying problems that could cause trouble for your business? How can you possibly know someone after only a few minutes of interaction? The answer is: you can't.

The Friend Who Almost Wasn't

When we were auditioning hosts for *Blue's Clues,* it was all too easy to make assumptions based on first impressions, but those assumptions weren't always right. One day, a young man walked into the studio. His hair was shaggy and he was carrying a skateboard under his arm. He wore ripped jeans and high-top sneakers and a T-shirt with a symbol for some band I didn't recognize. He had that typical bored skater boy expression and sauntered in as if he owned the place.

None of us thought he could be a good fit for the host of a show for preschoolers — parents would freak out, we thought — but we put him through the process anyway. We interviewed him, we looked at his résumé, and then we gave him a screen test. That's when it all turned around.

Steve Burns turned out to be exactly the person we needed for the role. He looked into the camera with such warmth and connection that he gave me the chills. This was our guy! His caring and authenticity were so obvious that we knew right then that we had found the missing link that would make the show a success. With a haircut and that signature green striped polo shirt, the quirky, friendly companion to Blue was born. It just goes to show you that if we had not suspended our preconceptions, we and millions of kids might have missed out on Steve.

The truth is, it's easier for us to drop the people we meet into predetermined categories. In an effort to understand the world around us, we categorize, group, label, but this very act often inhibits understanding. It is also unkind — akin to erecting a barrier in front of someone so you can't really see them. It's like saying, "Don't bother showing me who you are. I already know" — when, of course, you don't.

Choosing not to judge someone is kind because it opens a space for that person to be who they truly are, gives them an opportunity to be vulnerable, to share their true selves. Giving the kindness of non-judgment to another can also help broaden your perspective on the encounters you have with others, opening up possibilities and making room for genuine connection. When you see others with patience and openness rather than preconceptions and judgments, you develop a new level of compassion for the ideas and struggles and the basic identity of other human beings. This doesn't mean you have to agree with everything another person says, or even like that person. But radical kindness isn't about agreeing or disagreeing, liking or disliking. It's about living from a foundation of kindness, compassion, and respect 24/7.

The Unkindness of Jumping to Conclusions

This brings to mind something a friend of mine recently experienced on the subway late at night. He was sitting across from a homeless man who had no shoes. When a gang of teenagers boarded the train, my friend became nervous, especially when the teens began to taunt the homeless man, making fun of his bare feet. But then something amazing happened. The teenagers stopped and seemed to really *see.* To my friend's astonishment, one of the boys sat down next to the homeless man, took off his own shoes, peeled off his socks, and handed them to the man. The boys left the train, and the homeless man, who was probably as surprised as my friend, put the socks over his battered feet and smiled. My friend realized that he had made assumptions about those boys that were wrong — the boys were kinder than they at first seemed, more giving than my friend expected them to be, and could see with their hearts.

So, instead of jumping to conclusions, remember to hit Pause and notice — look for clues when you are tempted to assume. And remind yourself that you are always limited in what you can know about another human being. Even the brightest, most intelligent person cannot ever fully know someone else.

When you meet someone, the kindest thing to do is give them the benefit of the doubt — not necessarily assuming everything about them is perfect, not putting yourself in danger or being naïve, but just holding space for them to show you who they really are, with the recognition that getting to know a person takes time and insight. In the absence of real information, remember that good old Golden Rule and try to see someone the way *you* would want to be seen.

As you go through your life, see if you can think a little more deeply about the people you meet. Start by noticing the assumptions you make when you meet someone. What is your first impression? See if you can put it into words. Then challenge your assumptions by asking yourself, "How well do I know this person, really?" The answer is usually enough for you to take a small step back.

People are complex. Every human being is a universe unto himself. You may never get a chance to really visit that universe, but it is always better to assume that it is a benevolent one. Keep an open mind and, even better, an open heart. Whether it is a casual encounter or an official introduction, ask questions and listen actively to the answers. Remember the strategies from chapter 9: quiet your own ideas, make eye contact, and use your body language to indicate that you are paying attention. Try to learn one thing that goes against your initial judgment. You may not meet a kindred spirit, but you just may avoid missing out on a genuine human connection.

11
Assume the Best

Defusing Conflict with Kindness

We can learn a lot about kindness from kids. I once heard a story about a preschooler who was known for causing problems in the classroom. He often talked out of turn, threw tantrums, and got out of his seat when he wasn't supposed to. His teacher, normally a gentle, affectionate young woman, had run out of patience. She had tried redirecting, asking nicely, asking sternly, lecturing. Finally, one day, when the little boy began to throw yet another tantrum, she crossed her arms and said, "All right. That's it. You do *not* get a hug today."

This stopped the little boy in his tracks. He looked up at his teacher with a heartbroken expression and, through sobs and hiccups, said, "But that's all I wanted the whole time."

How ironic that we so often withhold the one thing people need from us the most. Granted, children can try our patience, and it is often easy for us to pass judgment on others when we're not in their particular situation, but it wasn't until this teacher accidentally exposed the child's pain that he was able to express his heartfelt need. And in the end, the teacher did what any good teacher — or, for that matter, anyone who practices radical kindness — would do once the line of communication was opened. She listened, noticed the boy's vulnerability, heart-saw his very human need to be nurtured, and gave him that hug he wanted. It took her only a matter of seconds to register all that was going on and take proper action.

Kindness had always been at her disposal, the way it is always at anyone's disposal at any time of the day. It doesn't take much effort to express, if we can only get past our initial reactions of frustration or irritation. We just need the tools and the awareness to practice it.

Conflict is inevitable, but dealing with it effectively is a skill that many people have not learned. It is easier to meet conflict with anger than with kindness. As with every other aspect of radical kindness we've talked about so far, meeting conflict with kindness requires both awareness and practice — and a bit of self-restraint.

When you're in conflict with someone, and think the other person is acting irrationally, use kindness to defuse the power of the conflict rather than escalate it. First of all, assume the best of the other person. If you can't quite find the space to heart-see them, at least pause and recognize what you actually know about the person's motivations. Make space for curiosity rather than judgment, and try not to react. There's nothing to be gained by escalating conflict.

This requires, first and foremost, deep respect for humanity — the person you're in conflict with is, after all, a member of the human race. Now take that respect for humanity and extend it to the specific person and situation at hand. This can require having an almost detached awareness of the conflict, and not taking it personally. This will be difficult. After all, the last thing you may want to do in the face of an angry, irrational person is help them, or be kind to them, or even see them at all. In fact, all you can see is red! But if you see with your heart and assume the best of the other person, you may discover that their anger, their argumentativeness, is a cry for help, an explosion of frustration, one that might stem from deep-seated fear. Maybe it's just carelessness. Whatever the cause of the conflict, when you assume the best about the other person, it is easier for you to be more forgiving and to defuse the conflict.

When I was growing up, we often ate stuffed artichokes during the holidays. My mother used to say that when we peeled back the layers of this odd-looking flower, we'd get to the heart. So, too, with conflict: when we take the time to peel back the layers of circumstance and suffering a person might be experiencing at any given time, we get to the heart of the matter and to the heart of the person.

Ultimately, we would all be better off in life if we assumed the best of others, if we understood that what we see in a conflict (rudeness, anger, frustration) might actually be symptoms of some deeper pain, suffering, stress, or unfulfilled need. That little boy throwing a tantrum in class just needed to be acknowledged; he needed an act of love. But he masked that need with bad behavior.

It Takes Two to Tango

Remember that all conflicts have at least two sides. The little boy was being difficult, but the teacher wasn't seeing. When you're having a conflict with someone, assume the best of the other person, but also turn the mirror on yourself and ask, "How am I contributing to this conflict?" You may be surprised at the extent to which you're helping to escalate the problem.

It's hard to recognize that you might be part of a conflict — but it's also empowering. While you can't change others, you can certainly change yourself. In that moment of irritation, frustration, anger, or fear, ask yourself what you can do to turn things around. To be radically kind is not only to assume the best about the person who is being difficult, but also to heart-see yourself, to discover what *you* can stop doing.

An attitude where we assume the best in others takes time to cultivate. It may seem hard to do in the heat of the moment, and let's face it, sometimes people are so rude that they may not be able to receive an act of kindness from you. But that doesn't mean you shouldn't extend one. Radical kindness isn't about what we get back from others. It's about acting from a place of respect and compassion for the other, regardless of whether we receive respect and compassion in return. And respect and compassion are often enough to defuse the conflicts around us.

Channel Your Inner Glinda

When you find yourself in a conflict, pay attention to your feelings. Pause, and then look and listen with your heart. Channel your inner Glinda. She might have something wise to say about how to handle the situation. She may gently show you that you aren't seeing something important, either about yourself or the other person. She may offer words of kindness to change the trajectory of the situation. Don't listen to the Wicked Witch and all the nasty things she is tempting you to say or think — about how wronged you are, how much more valid your opinions are. You don't need to engage. Instead, see how the other person is feeling. Have you ever felt that way? Can you empathize, even if you truly believe the other person to be wrong?

When you meet conflict with compassion, and a willingness to see the humanity you share with the other person, the alchemy of kindness can transform agitated, elevated feelings into calm, reasonable ones. To do this means letting down your guard a bit, being vulnerable so that the other person can feel safe letting down theirs. To be sure, this takes courage, but it can cool down emotions that risk coming to a boil.

Make a Peace Offering

Filmmaker and documentarian Ken Burns illustrated the idea of assuming the best in others when recounting a traffic incident he had recently been involved in. He was driving on Interstate 95, which runs along the length of the East Coast and where there are frequent tollbooths. Burns got into a situation where he had to cut in front of another car. The driver of the other car was furious. As Burns told me, "This guy leaned on his horn and gave me the middle finger, and I was waving at him to say, 'Sorry, sorry, sorry,' and he begrudgingly let me in, but he was obviously not happy about it." To defuse the tension even more, Burns felt that a small act of kindness was in order. When he pulled up to the tollbooth, where the toll was fifty cents, he gave the toll collector a dollar and said, "This is for me and the guy behind me" — a peace offering. Then he drove off as quickly as he could, hoping to avoid further trouble.

A few miles down the road, the guy caught up with him and waved, a big smile on his face. His anger was gone — evaporated, like magic. Burns went home and told his wife about the incident. "I realized I could have met anger with anger. I could have given him the middle finger back, but instead, I responded with a gesture of peace instead of conflict, and that man didn't seem to remember he had ever been angry. He looked purely happy. And I thought, we can all make those gestures of kindness as responses to gestures of anger. We can pull the fuel rods of anger and division right out and replace them with kindness, which is an understanding of how much alike we all are and how much we all need kindness to sustain us." Burns could have met anger with anger. Instead, he chose another path, and it cost him only fifty cents.

There are as many ways to meet gestures of anger with gestures of kindness as there are reasons to be angry. However you respond, try to give of yourself instead of taking from the other person. Notice your impulse to escalate the conflict, and think of more creative ways to respond. A conflict is a time for giving, not receiving. That can be difficult to accept, especially in the heat of the moment, but learning to think of confrontation differently can be transformative. As Mister Rogers once said, "There is no normal life that is free of pain. It's the very wrestling with our problems that can be the impetus for our growth."*

* Fred Rogers, *You Are Special: Words of Wisdom for All Ages from a Beloved Neighbor* (New York: Viking, 1994). Also available online at https://www.newsweek.com/fred-rogers-birthday-quotes-wont-you-be-my-neighbor-movie-854013.

▪ ▪ ▪ ▪

So, the next time someone acts with anger, whether it is a child having a meltdown in the grocery store or a partner snapping at you after a bad day, pause and look closer. What might that person really need? Is it attention? Is it a good listener? Is it empathy? Is it just for you to get out of the way so they can get somewhere on time? If you don't know for sure, assume the best. Then act from your increased awareness of the situation and from kindness rather than anger. Meet the conflict with a kind gesture, a humble admission, an anger-defusing smile, an acknowledgment of the other person's emotion, or an apology for your own.

In any conflict, you have a choice. You can choose to escalate the situation, you can choose to walk away from the situation, or you can choose to be kind. As the Dalai Lama once said, “Be kind whenever possible. It is always possible.”

■ ■ ■ ■

IV
Radical Kindness for a Better World

■ ■ ■ ■

12
SPEAK THE COMMON LANGUAGE OF KINDNESS

HEART-SEEING THE "OTHER"

Kindness isn't always easy, especially if you are confronted with someone whose culture, perspective, opinions, beliefs, or manner of living you vehemently oppose. How do you heart-see the "other" — that person who is not like you; that person who makes you uncomfortable, who makes you bristle; the one you've heard stories about, maybe in the news or on the Internet; the one you don't know at all but are sure you wouldn't like. Maybe it's a politician, or a religious figure, or a celebrity. Maybe it's someone who voted for the other guy in a recent election. Or maybe it's someone from a completely different culture, who acts in a way you don't understand. After working in children's television programming for more than twenty years, I often derive my understanding of life, my inspiration, my answers, from sources familiar to children. In this instance, an old fairy tale comes to mind.

SEEING THE "PRINCE" INSIDE THE "BEAST"

When I think about how to deal with difficult people, I think of "Beauty and the Beast." The Beast is angry and mean, argumentative and cruel. But the curse that changed him into the Beast was, in fact, placed on him because of his inability to be kind to someone else. The Beast is a beast because he couldn't be kind.

Belle is kind. Seeing with her heart, she is able to see past the Beast's rude and cruel behavior to the sad eyes and the humanity deep within. The kindness within the Beast is just an ungerminated seed, but Belle sees it nevertheless, and it is only because of her kind and loving reaction to the Beast that he is able to learn the meaning of love and kindness and break the curse, becoming a prince once again.

Those of us living in the real world, of course, see the problematic elements of this story. Are we supposed to submit to cruel behavior? Are we supposed to let ourselves be hurt, insulted, abused? No way. Part of being kind to yourself is to be your own advocate in the face of cruel behavior, and another part of being kind is to protect the vulnerable.

But there is an aspect to this story that is on point: the behavior we may abhor in others is a product of that person's past, their poor choices, or, in many cases, pain that others inflicted upon them. If we look deeper at other people — at those who hurt us, whom we're inclined to dismiss, or even whom we actively dislike — what we see may soften our reactions toward them. Many people out in the world act like the Beast (school bullies, difficult bosses, other drivers), but instead of rousing the rest of the village to take up their torches and pitchforks, we have the choice to pause, look closer, and try to see the prince within — or, if not the prince, than at least a lonely, fearful, sad, or lost person.

CHANNEL YOUR INNER CHILD

We are all born to be kind. Children don't want to "kill the Beast."

They want to understand him. Where adults often jump to conclusions, children are curious. Where adults often revile the "other," children are fascinated by differences, unoffended by coarseness, and interested in connection. Think of how a child sees someone they've never met. Without a lifetime of accumulated opinions and prejudices, they see more purely what is in front of them. They want to explore the other's face with their hands. They want to touch the wrinkles or the strange hair or the gnarled hands. They shamelessly point and ask questions:

"Why is that lady's hair white?"

"Why doesn't that man have an arm?"

"Is that a boy or a girl?"

When a child looks at someone else with wonder and curiosity, they are seeing from the heart. They don't lead with hate. They want to touch the Beast's fur, ask about his fangs. And while a child may hide from the Beast's roar, they will always want to know why he's roaring.

Adults aren't always as inquisitive as we should be; we are usually focused elsewhere. There are responsibilities to meet, bills to pay, aging parents to help, distracted children to get to school, and all the stress that comes from living in a world that can be beastly in its own way. Though we were all once children, at some point we stop looking at the world around us with wonder, relying instead on old, preformed opinions. But the moment we stop asking questions, we stop heart-seeing, and that is the moment we lose out on opportunities to see a bigger world and to forge deeper connections with the people around us.

DISSENTING OPINION

I was always inspired by the decades-long friendship between Supreme Court justices Ruth Bader Ginsburg and Antonin Scalia. These two could not have been more politically opposite. Even so, they were close friends who socialized and, along with their spouses, spent holidays together. Each sustained an enduring respect for the other. Judge Ginsburg said that Judge Scalia's dissenting opinions always made her a better judge because he was sharp and pointed out any weak spots in her arguments. Neither made assessments about the other's humanity based on political opinion. Each saw beyond the external to the human being beneath.

We can learn a lot from their example. Justices Ginsburg and Scalia's friendship endured because it contained the hallmarks of radical kindness: the ability to actively listen, to notice the other and acknowledge their differences; the ability to refrain from judging each other even when they disagreed.

That's right. They were two of the most powerful judges in the United States, and yet they did not judge each other.

But what if the person you encounter is not as civil as a Supreme Court justice? There are loud, outwardly nasty, obnoxious, selfish, rude, and irresponsible people in the world. But even those people are human beings, each one on his own path. They have their reasons for thinking and acting the way they do, and whether you like their thoughts and actions is not the point. To see from the heart and to lead with kindness in all things means to accept the fact that every living human being deserves to be treated with dignity and respect.

Period. As someone with hot Italian blood that can rise above the boiling point, I know firsthand that it's not easy to lead with kindness. But when we come from a place where we honor all individuals, we not only open new lines of communication, without that defensiveness that occurs when two sides are quarreling, but we also advance to new levels of compassion and understanding. Whether we are talking one on one, political party to political party, or nation to nation, arguing will almost surely *not* convert the other person to your point of view.

This is where radical kindness can have an even more profound impact, not just on you but on everyone for whom you model it. To default to kindness all the time means defaulting to kindness even in the most difficult scenarios. When discourse becomes heated, or when you find yourself lying awake worrying about someone else's political or religious opinion, then you have a problem. There is a difference between disagreeing with an opinion or action and disagreeing with the very nature of the other person. Remember that you can't ever truly know the inner nature of another, nor are you ever fully aware of the baggage you yourself carry that is blocking your vision, so you have no basis on which to judge another human being's essential self.

A better inroad is to meet people where they are in life. Don't expect to change someone. Don't pretend you can mind-read or truly know something about another person you can't possibly know. And don't wish someone to be different from who they are at that moment. We do others a disservice by disrespecting their thoughts and feelings, and we cause unneeded stress in our own lives by wanting reality to be different from what it is.

You can take action to support your political, religious, or personal beliefs without demeaning another person's humanity. You can even object to the way someone is performing a role or job, and work to replace that person without being unkind. There is nothing unkind about advocating for a cause you believe in, provided that you don't infringe on the rights and liberties of others. Radical kindness in action means working for your own beliefs even as you respect the humanity of everyone with whom you are in opposition.

Debating 101

It is natural to want to be with like-minded people, but you won't always be surrounded by people who think the way you do. The world is filled with "others." But if you can approach them with childlike curiosity and a desire to look beyond the borders of your own experience or opinions, you will open your mind to learning from those who come from other backgrounds and whose opinions are different from your own.

We can always use our hearts to dig deeper, to find a connection, and to celebrate rather than degrade the differences we see, even when they offend us. We can always debate respectfully, even when others don't. How do you do this?

- Imagine there is a judge keeping score or that you are being graded on your skills.
- Stay calm. Be direct and respectful. This can help you keep your emotions in check. You don't win a debate by yelling or insulting. You win by

making the most cogent points.

- Actively argue your point, but actively listen, too.
- If the emotional temperature starts to rise . . . pause. Wait. Remember your commitment to practicing kindness.
- When it's your turn to speak, stay on topic. Don't make it personal. Maybe you *can* teach the other person something. Attacking them for their perspective will never accomplish this. Remember: it takes just one person to take the high road, and suddenly the whole conversation becomes elevated, more civil.
- When it seems that the longed-for coming together is not go-

ing to happen, do the kindest thing possible for the other person and yourself: just walk away.

CURING "CULTURE SHOCK" WITH KINDNESS

There is another type of "other" that can present a barrier to radical kindness: someone from another culture whose language, behaviors, and practices are completely foreign to us. While it can be uncomfortable to be around people whose entire way of living is unfamiliar — this is why some people get "culture shock" while traveling — it is also a great opportunity.

When you come into direct contact with someone you don't "get," someone vastly different from you, whether they are from another country or hold a completely different ideology, do what you can to relax. Gently let your guard down, and allow yourself to be open and vulnerable. Actively listen to them. Be present for that person, even if you don't understand or agree with everything you see and hear. And when you aren't sure what to do next, remember that kindness is a common language.

Richard Wiese, president of the Explorers Club, a society dedicated to advancing scientific research around the globe, has traveled all over the world, to some of the remotest places on earth, lands vastly different from the Connecticut town where he lives. When asked about his experience, he said, "The more I travel around the world to cultures that are seemingly completely different than mine, the more I witness the importance of kindness. In many situations where there is a misunderstanding about the culture, one-sided or mutual, kindness can become the language of communication that brings people together again."

Wiese recalls visiting an oasis in the Atacama Desert, in Chile, where he shared a meal with the people living there, during a ceremony called the Flowering of the Llama, a kind of Thanksgiving for that culture. At first, he felt uncomfortable. The customs and celebrations were strange and unsettling to him. Then, out of the blue, a little girl popped up in front of him and said, " 'Hola!' as if he were an old friend she hadn't seen for a long time." Wiese talked with the little girl for a while, and began to feel more at home. The more time he spent with the villagers, the more he could see through what was foreign about them and into what he had in common with them: "For people who do not have much, to share their food with strangers — that is like me giving my car to someone to keep. It's a big deal. I realized that even though these people had customs I didn't understand, we all understood the language of kindness."

When young children encounter the world for the first time, everything is new to them. For adults who travel, the experience is the same: they're coming upon new people, cultures, accents, languages, practices, rituals, and points of view for the first time. This is excellent practice for honing tolerance and understanding differences. In his book *The Innocents Abroad,* Mark Twain wrote, "Travel is fatal to prejudice, bigotry, and narrow-mindedness, and many of our people need it sorely on these accounts. Broad, wholesome, charitable views of men and things cannot be acquired by vegetating in one little corner of the earth all one's lifetime." The more you see, the more you can know, and the more differences you are exposed to, the more tolerant and understanding you will become.

The Power of "Touchstones"

If accepting the "other" feels too difficult for you, find something to anchor you, to remind you to defer to keeping your heart open. I keep a small heart-shaped stone in my pocket. Whenever I feel I might go in the wrong direction and say or do something that isn't kind, I reach for that stone. Then I feel grounded, and I get right back on track. Having something solid and real is a reminder to pause, think before I speak, listen without interrupting, and stay open to all possible ways of being.

Peaceful interactions can feel elusive, but when we change our perspective, see with our hearts, and approach interactions with calm rationality and open-hearted kindness, we may be surprised at how much easier it is to communicate. Barriers may fall away. Anger may fade. Common ground may emerge where you least expect it. When it comes to reaching across the aisle, kindness may be exactly the remedy our world needs.

13
Kindness Without Credit

Anonymous Kindness for a More Giving World

Let's face it. When someone gives us credit for being kind or doing the right thing, it feels really good. Praise, or even just the feeling of doing the right thing, often creates physical, mental, and emotional rewards, all of which are reinforced by a rush of dopamine and the other "happy hormones" that are released when we act kindly. But anonymous kindness can produce its own rich rewards, even though not taking or getting credit for what we do doesn't come naturally to most of us. When we give without any thought of receiving anything in return, we experience a new level of freedom and selflessness.

Think about it from the receiver's point of view: When someone does something nice for you, you feel an obligation to act in kind. But when you don't know who did you the kindness, you have no obligation. You are free to enjoy it without any thought of paying it back. It's a whole different feeling that can be so rewarding that you may want to pass it along, pay it forward, by doing something kind for someone else. This is how kindness grows and snowballs and causes bigger, more significant changes.

THE ALTRUISTIC DONOR CHAIN

A study published in *The New England Journal of Medicine* looked at what the researchers called a "nonsimultaneous, extended, altruistic donor chain." They cited the example of a man who decided to donate a kidney to a random person in need, a woman he didn't know. The husband of the woman who received the man's kidney (who had wanted to donate one of his own kidneys to his wife, but had an incompatible blood type) was so moved by the donor's act that he decided to do the same for a woman whose mother could not donate to her because *her* blood type was incompatible. *That* woman's mother was a better match for another person who needed a kidney, so she donated to *that* person. And on and on it went, from anonymous person to anonymous person, altruistic donor to altruistic donor, until ten people had new kidneys, and in most cases, they didn't know the donor.

Of course, you don't have to give up an internal organ to make a profound anonymous impact on someone's life. There are many small acts you can perform, and nobody has to know. If you find out that someone is struggling to pay an electric bill or get their car repaired or meet their child's preschool tuition in a lean month, you could cover the cost, and ask to remain anonymous. You could leave a gift for someone in a nursing home or take school supplies to a child who needs them; just leave them in the school office with an anonymous note to the parents. You could take pet supplies to an animal shelter, send a gift to a soldier overseas, donate blood, pay for someone's coffee, or, as Ken Burns did, pay the toll for the driver in the car behind yours.

There are also many ways to practice secret kindnesses without spending a cent. In a speech, Nelson Mandela once said, "There can be no greater gift than that of giving one's time and energy to help another without expecting anything in return." In the spirit of those words, do one anonymous kindness and then bask in the warmth of that feeling for the rest of the day. Pick up something sharp you see lying in the street, so no one gets a flat tire. Clean up trash in a school parking lot. Get up early to shovel an elderly neighbor's driveway or mow their lawn when they're not at home.

Throw a Sandal on the Tracks

I'm reminded of a story about Gandhi. He was running to catch a train that had already left the station. The people in the third-class section of the train (where Gandhi always rode) recognized him and reached out to help him aboard, but as they pulled him into the train car, one of his sandals fell off and down onto the tracks.

Everyone stared for a moment. What could they do? There was no time to jump off the train, run to the sandal, pick it up, and run back. The train was moving too quickly. As for Gandhi, he seemed unbothered by this turn of events. Safely aboard, he took off his other sandal and heaved it as far as he could, back in the direction he'd come.

The people on the train couldn't believe their eyes, and asked him, "Mahatma, why would you throw your other sandal out there?"

Gandhi answered, "Whoever finds that first sandal, wouldn't it be nice if they found the other one as well?"

Instead of worrying about not having any sandals, Gandhi was thinking about the person who might find his one lone sandal on the tracks. That person might need a pair of sandals. But what good would one sandal be to such a person? Gandhi knew he would never get credit for his act, and he didn't want it. He projected his heart into the future and acted from a place of concern for a stranger he'd probably never meet.

There are always opportunities to "throw a sandal on the tracks." Instead of thinking about what you see in front of you, practice thinking about what, and whom, you *don't* see. Think about who might come along next, who might need something they wouldn't dare ask for. This takes some creativity, an ability to heart-see what isn't there, to imagine what isn't obvious, and to know how to act when there is no clear directive. To open your mind.

When you go to the grocery store, you could pick up some food to take to the food bank, for people whom you will probably never meet but who are hungry right now. If you see trash in a park, think about the kids who might come to play there later, or the wildlife that might ingest something harmful, mistaking it for food. You can't actually see those kids or that flock of ducks, but you can see the trash and imagine the impact it could have later.

There are many ways to "throw a sandal on the tracks" in your own life, to reach out with kindness to that which is unseen or hasn't happened yet. One small act could trigger another, which could trigger another, until the future is a better place than the present. To quote my old friend and current U.S. senator from New Jersey Cory Booker, "We can never allow our inability to do *everything* undermine our determination to do *something.*" You may never know how a small act of kindness impacts another's life — and you know what? That's okay.

You've done something that has the potential to change a person's life for the better, even if they never know it or never get the chance to thank you. And, really, that's acknowledgment enough.

14
Changing the World One Kindness at a Time

As I look into the future and imagine the ways that any one person might change the world, I continue to circle back to our children. It has been my life's work to understand the world from a child's point of view, to be an advocate for children, and to instill hope for the future through lessons of kindness to children. Because of my immersion in this world, I believe I have a perspective I might not have had if I had taken a different career path.

Let Life Be the Treasure You Seek

One of the greatest lessons I've learned over the years is that what you seek determines your path. In Paulo Coelho's *The Alchemist,* we go on a journey with Santiago, a shepherd not much older than a boy, who sells his flock in search of treasure. His journey leads him through obstacle after obstacle, as he continually seeks but never finds this great treasure he imagines will change his life. But he does find the alchemist, who shares his wisdom about what is essentially the meaning of life. The alchemist tells Santiago that life itself is the treasure. Life, love, the quest for truth, and our own experiences — these are more valuable than any material treasure anyone could ever find. Santiago learns to see and listen with his heart, and ultimately, he follows his heart's desires in order to live his dream. In the end, he realizes that what the alchemist said is true: "Remember that wherever your heart is, there you will find your treasure." This reminder can help us all seek what is truly valuable.

We are all on this journey of life together, and sometimes it is hard to know what the real treasure is. The sparkly, shiny things — more money, a nicer car, a bigger house, designer clothes, the promotion, the title, fame — look so much like treasure that it is easy to get distracted by them. But what good is shine and sparkle without affection and kindness?

What radical kindness can teach anyone who practices it is that real treasures, the ones that last and make us more generous and more giving, may be invisible, but they enrich our lives more than any material possession or worldly acknowledgment. By embodying kindness, you have the opportunity to spread it every day, triggering it in others again and again. One big gesture is nice, but a million little gestures over the course of a lifetime can have an impact that is vaster and far more enduring.

Mister Rogers's Most Radical Gift

This book began with a story about Fred Rogers, and I'd like to share another story about the man who was a treasure not just to me but to millions of people. Though many saw him as a simple man with simple ideas, he was a true human embodiment of kindness, living it every day in a way that reached far beyond the people he knew personally, and in a way that actually helped change the world and improve the future.

Episode 1663 of *Mister Rogers' Neighborhood* aired after the assassination of Dr. Martin Luther King Jr. During this time in our country's history, racial tensions were high, and the Jim Crow South was reluctant to change. One of the battlegrounds for racial equality was the country's public swimming pools and beaches, which African Americans were often blocked from using. Both sides protested, staging demonstrations outside public pools that sometimes ended in police violence and arrest. Some whites even took the drastic step of pouring bleach into pools where African Americans were trying to swim.

Of course, the issue of segregated pools was too politically charged to discuss on a program aimed at preschoolers. Yet Fred Rogers saw that the issue needed his attention. He had convinced a man named François Clemmons, a successful opera singer and a descendant of slaves and sharecroppers, to play the singing policeman Officer Clemmons. In this particular episode, Mister Rogers is seen sitting in the front yard of his television "house," soaking his bare feet in a kiddie pool. It is a hot day, and Mister Rogers explains to the children watching that he is cooling off by putting his feet in the water. When Officer Clemmons passes by, Mister Rogers invites him to sit down and cool off his feet. Officer Clemmons agrees. He sits down next to Mister Rogers, takes off his shoes and socks, and puts his feet into the cold water. As they sit there, the camera moves down to show two light-colored feet and two dark-colored feet together in that kiddie pool. Then it pulls back to show Mister Rogers glancing up at the camera, as if to be sure his point is being made.

To many children, this was a simple instance of neighborhood camaraderie — but just imagine the implication for any child feeling personally affected by the events of the day. Imagine a child who had been banned from a swimming pool, or one who was allowed in but not allowed to bring along a black friend. This small gesture of kindness, of inclusivity, on that episode of *Mister Rogers' Neighborhood* sent a big message to children watching about what was the right thing to do.

Any neighbor could share Mister Rogers's pool. Color was irrelevant. By his simple act of fairness, of basic human decency, Mister Rogers did a kindness for the world — he demonstrated that equality is normal. He gave every child of every color watching that episode an example of what it means to love another, to be kind to one's neighbor, and to share the common experience of cooling off on a hot day. This is how kindness can change the world — when it becomes the norm.

BEING KIND EVEN WHEN IT'S HARD

One step at a time, by enacting kindnesses as a matter of course — kindnesses to ourselves, to our loved ones, to strangers, to nations — we can do our part as a member of the human community. Sometimes it's frustrating. Sometimes it's hard. Sometimes it even seems impossible. "Life is difficult," psychologist M. Scott Peck once wrote in his famous best seller *The Road Less Traveled.* "This is a great truth, one of the greatest truths. It is a great truth because once we truly see this truth, we transcend it."

I will admit I sometimes have trouble transcending the truth Dr.

Peck talks about. Sometimes I dream that we could all live in Neverland, a place where nobody has to grow up; a place without the complicated problems of the adult world; where life is a game, full of exciting adventures; where we can sleep in tree houses, cavort with mermaids and pixies, and outsmart pirates. Wouldn't it be lovely if we could all live in a place where good is good and bad is bad, where there are no gray areas, no moral conundrums, no political arguments or family squabbles or jobs or money or any of the things that complicate life in the real world? If we could all share the "swimming pool" that is the world without conflict, life would be so much easier.

But the world is fraught with peril, stress, responsibility, and frustration. But it is also filled with beauty, love, connection, ease, fun, play, learning, experience, wonder, and kindness. You just have to look at it with the eyes of your inner child: at the bright, bold colors of flowers; at the grandeur of mountain ranges; at New York City at night; at the vastness of a cloudless sky; at groups of people coming together in love and solidarity for a common cause. We need to keep that inner child at the forefront of all we do — not buried deep within, where she cannot get out, but right up front, where she can help guide us through the journey of life that is, after all, the ultimate treasure.

This, in the end, is the real secret to radical kindness: To carry within you the open heart of a child, but to use that openness and natural-born kindness in ways only an adult has the power to do. To refine it. Grow it. Strive to better understand it. Use it to look more deeply into yourself, to reach out more actively to others, and to take on the responsibility of making this world a better place for everyone, now and far into the future. Embody it in all you see and all you do. Show it to others so they can take up the charge and spread it even further.

There will always be parts of us that get swept up in the tangled web of the world, in moments when we are tempted to act unkindly, to argue, to hide our true selves from the ones we love. But when your essential self is set free, it can take your hand and remind you that, when in doubt, all you have to do is pause, take a deep breath, smile, look, be gentle . . . and choose kindness.

Let's persist in seeing ourselves and others with our hearts, make an agreement to be better every day through acts of kindness toward all the world — its people, its animals, and its environment. Let's spread radical kindness to every corner of the wide world, one kind act at a time. Let's preserve our future by nurturing our children so that they can grow up to continue the mission of creating a kinder world. This is how we will evolve: by striving to see rightly and embracing what is invisible to the eye but essential to the heart.

15
Thirty-Two Acts of Radical Kindness You Could Do Today

"Can you help me?" Our four magic words are the inspiration for this list of kind acts anyone can do as they seek to embody radical kindness each day. These thirty-two acts of kindness can put you on the road to establishing kindness as your default perspective. Start today, and remember: this list is only a beginning. As you internalize radical kindness, you'll find yourself getting increasingly creative in expressing it, both inwardly and outwardly.

Some of the items here are big, and some are small. Some require deeper heart-seeing, while others may be easier to manage. Peruse this list and choose from it randomly; or work through it in order, to continue to hone your radical kindness practice. Or choose those that you know you can do at this stage of your journey, and aspire to do later those that seem more challenging. Adventures await you as you explore the many possibilities for kindness.

1. Keep with You a Token from Your Childhood.

Carrying a concrete reminder of who you were as a child can help you stay in touch with your authentic self, that person you were when you were unguarded and wholly yourself. A small keepsake or toy, a picture you drew, a letter you wrote, or even a grammar school photo can be inspirational. Whenever you feel you're losing touch with or straying from your authentic self, pull out this token and look at it. Touch it. Tell yourself, "This is still me. Be kind to this child."

2. Phone a Friend.

You know that friend who knows you better than anyone? When you need to feel better about who you are, call them up or meet them for lunch or a coffee. Just being with someone who loves you and really understands you can help you feel more loving and understanding toward yourself. If such a wonderful friend can love you, then you can love you, too.

3. Make Your Favorite Meal.

If you are prone to telling yourself that you don't deserve something, whether it's as general as an indulgence or as specific as a certain number of calories, it's time to get cooking! Food is one of our most primal needs, and one of our most primal pleasures. Allowing yourself the indulgence of food you truly love can feed your soul as well as your body. Prepare it lovingly, sit down at an actual table, use nice dishes, maybe light a candle, and savor every glorious bite of that macaroni and cheese, that juicy steak with mashed potatoes, that chocolate cake with ice cream, or whatever it is that makes your soul hum. If you aren't one for cooking, go to a favorite restaurant — maybe the one you save for birthdays and other special occasions — for no other reason than to send yourself the message that today you have chosen to feed yourself well, on all levels.

4. Smile at Yourself in the Mirror. We can be so cruel to ourselves when we look in the mirror, zeroing in on every imperfection. It's time to give your mirror experience a makeover by standing in front of one and heart-seeing yourself, looking past your physical body and into your heart. Find your beauty. Keep looking until you see all that is good and right and lovable about yourself. It's in there, I promise. When you see it, give yourself a big, wide, joyful smile. A smile is kindness to another — but with a mirror, you can give that kindness to yourself.

5. Go for a Walk.

It's funny (or not so funny) how we can spend entire days sitting in front of a computer when a deadline looms or just because it's what our job requires. But the human body is meant to move! Without movement, your circulation slows, your digestion slows, your breathing gets shallower, and your muscles get stiffer. So, be kind to your body: get up from that desk and take a walk. You don't need to run or sprint or lift weights or even sweat if you don't feel like it. Just walking, especially outside in the fresh air, is a kindness to your spirits as well as to the body you call home.

6. Go Barefoot Outside.

Speaking of walking outside, you might as well take off your shoes and socks! There is a practice called "earthing" that is based on the theory that your body can take energy from the earth if you stand on it with bare feet. When you are feeling sluggish, slow, tired, or just sapped of energy, connecting with the planet might be just what you need. Give yourself the kindness of a natural energy boost. Proponents of earthing say that it makes you feel happier and healthier, restoring your depleted resources so you can feel better and do better for yourself and others. All you have to do is take off your shoes and socks, head outside, and stand in the grass, the dirt, on a rock, on the sand, or in seawater, to charge your batteries and feel like yourself again. Added bonus: going barefoot can remind you of your childhood. Let yourself feel that feeling again, of walking through soft grass or wet sand or even the sun-warmed concrete of a sidewalk. (Another natural practice you can try is *shinrin-yoku,* or "forest bathing," a Japanese tradition that involves nothing more than walking through a forest or natural area with a lot of trees. The idea is that trees emit compounds that are good for human health, whether it's the oxygen or the natural oils diffused from evergreens. According to several studies, forest bathing boosts the immune system; lowers blood pressure; reduces stress hormones; improves mood; increases focus, including in children with ADHD; accelerates recovery from injury or illness; increases energy; and helps improve sleep quality. Look for nature trails, parks, or any public wooded area near you, or take advantage of tree-filled areas when you travel.)

7. Create a New Daily Ritual.

Do something small for yourself every day, such as taking two minutes to stretch every morning upon waking, having one square of chocolate every day at 3:00 p.m., or ending every day with a cup of warm peppermint tea. It can be anything that makes you feel good. Do it consistently and keep it sacred. In fact, when you get busy, make it the last thing you bump off your schedule, because that is when you'll need it the most.

8. Get That Physical.

It's always a good idea to keep tabs on your health, even if it's only to get baseline measurements of your blood pressure, blood sugar, cholesterol, and vitamin D levels, so you can take action if anything changes. If you do find a problem, address it now to keep it from getting out of hand. Taking care of yourself is both an acknowledgment that you deserve to be healthy and a way to ensure you can remain fully present for the other people in your life.

9. Say No.

When did *no* become a bad word? Most of us are overworked, overscheduled, and overextended — and for what? If your schedule is too packed or you're too stressed, don't take on that thing you really don't want to do — even if it's something that seems kind, such as volunteering or working the school bake sale. Remember to put your own oxygen mask on first. If you can't handle something, say no and focus on tending to your own needs. Maybe later you'll be ready to take on something else, but when you aren't feeling up to it, it's okay to say, "I'm sorry. I just can't fit that in right now."

10. Look Up.

When life gets busy, overwhelming, or you don't feel well (whether mentally or physically), it's so easy to focus on the negative aspects of the situation that you lose perspective. Few things will help put your problems back into perspective like looking up. Throughout the course of your busy day or your busy night, take a minute to stop and tilt your head back. What color is the sky today? What are the clouds doing? Is a storm brewing? Are the stars out? Take a few deep breaths. Really gaze. Take it all in — that vast space. What's going on up there? What unfathomable chemistry, what unpredictable physics, and so much that is unknown? Think about how your problems fit into this boundless, infinite scope. Remember that you are the only one like you in all that endless space, that the stresses and problems you face will come and go, but in the end, they'll mean little — they are space dust. How lucky we all are to be here! How small we all are, and yet, how unique. Give yourself the profound kindness of considering your place in the universe and letting it serve as a way to wipe clean the day's slate and put your life in perspective.

11. Ask Someone, "Can You Help Me?"

Remember your work on being vulnerable. Open up and ask for help, whether for something physical ("Can you help me carry in these groceries?") or emotional ("Can you help cheer me up? I'm feeling down today"). Then don't forget to actually accept the help! Do someone else the kindness of being able to be there for you, to give you something you need that you can't give yourself.

12. Leave a Note.

Slip a sweet note of love, encouragement, or inspiration into your partner's pocket, your child's lunch, or a friend's purse or wallet when they aren't looking. Write someone a card or a short letter and mail it — in a real envelope, with an actual postage stamp. Or write an anonymous friendly note and leave it under a car's windshield to lift someone's spirits. Keep it upbeat, like, "Enjoy this beautiful day!" or offer a quick pep talk: "Yes you can!" or "Believe in yourself!"

13. Tell Somebody Something You Love about Them.

Some people rarely let themselves dwell on their own good qualities, especially those who tend to focus on helping others — their parents, their children, their friends. Give that person the gift of your insight into their most wonderful qualities. Avoid more superficial qualities such as "nice hair" or "pretty sweater," although those things are pleasing to hear, too. Instead, look for something you detect by heart-seeing your friend or family member. Is that person always gentle with others? An incurable optimist? Cheerful and sunny? Passionate about their interests? Deeply invested in the welfare of their children? Does that person have a great work ethic? A warm heart? Whatever you see, say it. It might come at a time when it is exactly what that person needs to hear to make it through the day.

14. Invite Someone to Something. Being invited to things makes people feel special. Whenever you extend an invitation — to a new acquaintance to your home for a cup of tea and a get-to-know-you chat; to a friend to go check out a local attraction you know would interest her; or to your child for a "date" out, just the two of you — you extend a kindness, you show the other person that you value their company and want to spend time with them. You have even more of a reason to do this if someone has already invited you out or had you over for dinner. Go ahead and reciprocate. Set a date for dinner or an informal get-together. Foster your connections.

15. Remember People.

Nobody likes that feeling of introducing themselves and then having the other person forget their name or some other essential aspect of them within minutes. Sure, we're all busy and scattered, but whenever you meet someone, a real kindness is to give them your full attention, take note of their name, and vow to remember it. (Use a mnemonic device if it helps you remember.) Then see if you can learn one new thing about that person that you'll remember and mention later, such as how they take their coffee, that they're a dog or a cat person, that they play soccer on weekends, or they're just back from Thailand. It's affirming and confidence-boosting when someone you've just met calls you by your name and asks you a personal question. "Hi, Jim. How is Scruffy doing after his vet visit?" or "Hey, Joan. I'm headed to the coffee machine; can I get one for you? Cream, no sugar, right?"

16. Smile at a Stranger.

Take a cue from small towns and smile at someone when you encounter them on the street or elsewhere during your day. No need to say anything — just offer a smile, a brief nod of acknowledgment that you are seeing a fellow human being in passing. Maybe even offer a "Good morning" to brighten that person's day. It's just about the easiest thing you can do that can really make a difference to another person.

17. Spend Fifteen Minutes Listening.

Active listening requires practice. Sit down with your partner, parent, child, or good friend and ask what's going on in their lives. Really listen. Ask questions to learn more. If they don't have much to say, be more specific. "How did your test go?" "Are you feeling better about your relationship with your sister?" "Tell me how that problem with your boss turned out." "I want to hear all about your vacation." Focus fully on what the other person is saying without interrupting or saying anything about yourself. Make sure you understand. Let them feel genuinely heard. They will feel good all day.

18. Do Something Considerate Just Because.

Bring flowers to your mom. Make your partner's favorite meal. Bring in the mail. Move your clothes out of the dryer right after it stops, so the next person to use the machine doesn't have to. Move your shoes out of the passageway where everybody walks. Put your dirty dishes in the dishwasher. Let the other driver take that parking spot you were both eyeing. Open the door for someone whose hands are full. Don't hold up traffic by driving in the passing lane. Wherever you go, look for more opportunities to do something for someone else just because it would make *their* life easier.

19. "Can I Get You Anything?"

Every time you go to the grocery store, the pharmacy, the discount store, the hardware store, to get coffee or lunch or takeout, or anywhere else to pick up something you need, ask others if you can get them anything. If you have a friend or neighbor who has a hard time getting to the store, offer to pick up something for them, even if you don't need to go there yourself.

20. Give up Your Seat.

On a bus, on a train, or in a busy waiting room, give up your seat to someone who looks like they could use it more than you. All too often, pregnant women, the elderly, and those with disabilities are forced to stand while able-bodied people sit. You can set an example for others by giving up your seat as often as possible. Others might catch the hint and start doing it themselves.

21. Volunteer.

Work for no money? Absolutely! Many organizations desperately need help but don't have the funds to pay people. Find a cause close to your heart — helping out at a soup kitchen, walking dogs and petting cats at an animal shelter, manning a crisis line, organizing donations at a food bank, delivering meals to people who can't leave their homes due to age or illness, reading to kids at a children's hospital, helping out at a homeless shelter or safe house, visiting older folks at a nursing home or a memory care unit, tutoring at the local grade school. Every community has needs. If you have kids, taking them with you to volunteer is a great learning experience for them.

22. Give More.

If you have the financial resources others don't, you have many opportunities to give people things they genuinely need. Buy a sandwich for a homeless person or give them a pair of socks or shoes, a warm coat, gloves, a hat, a scarf, or a warm blanket. Women would also appreciate a purse with feminine hygiene supplies inside; it's hard to find those on the street. On the next rainy day, take two umbrellas with you and give one to the first person you see caught out in the rain without one. Leave a book in a public place for someone else to find; or give one directly to a child you don't know. Or put the books you've already read or don't need anymore in one of those little "Free Library" boxes. The ones near schools get emptied quickly and are especially in need of books for young children and preteens. If you have the resources, every time you buy food, clothes, shoes, or toys, buy something extra to donate to someone in need, or to a food drive, clothing drive, toy drive, or a local organization that distributes these things to people in need. And never, ever pass up a lemonade stand without buying a cup from the local kids.

Be Kind for a Better World

23. Get Involved.

How much do you know about your local community? What are its needs, its biggest issues, greatest challenges? Are there issues with the local schools, environmental concerns, infrastructure problems? Is the community growing too quickly, or losing people? Do you need more bike trails/lanes, more support for law enforcement? Are there tensions between opposing groups over an issue, and can you help? Start getting more involved in your community so you feel more a part of where you live and more connected to the people around you. Even if it's just to join your building's co-op board or your neighborhood association, get to know your neighborhood better; go to those meetings. Or take it to the next level: go to your local town hall meetings. Are you getting all your news from the Internet? Try reading the local paper. Get to know your city council, your mayor, your state representatives and senators. When you find an issue you feel is important, help out. Support the candidates who are doing the work you believe in. Help get people to the polls to vote; or get involved with local groups working to make your community better. Maybe you could even run for a local position, to help make positive changes for the people who share your immediate environment.

24. Buy Local.

Local businesses often find it difficult to compete with big chain stores. Is it really worth saving a couple of dollars just to go to a big discount store when you could support your local businesses and keep your money in your own community? Shop at the local grocer, local bookstore, local toy store, and eat at the local restaurants. Go to the farmers' market, the local garden store, the local bakery, and get your coffee from the local coffee shop. While you're at it, get to know the shop owners and their challenges, and encourage others to shop locally, too. You could even challenge yourself to a week, a month, or a year of patronizing only local businesses for whatever you need, unless there is no local option. While you're at it, go online and write glowing reviews for your favorite local restaurant or shop on Yelp, Google, or other online review sites, to help bring in more business.

25. Be Kind to the Environment.

There are obvious ways to do your part to help the earth, such as recycling and not littering, but there are many other things you can do to help. Bring your own water bottle, rather than buying bottled water, to reduce one huge source of pollution. Buy a steel straw instead of using plastic straws, and bring your own reusable bags to the grocery store. Bring your own containers for food you buy from those bulk bins at the health food store. Pick up trash when you see it. Pitch in for local clean-up days in your community, or organize them yourself, with neighborhood kids — you could pick up the trash in a park or wildlife preserve, then have fun afterward. Every little thing you do to be kind to the earth could make a difference, but the greatest differences will happen when everyone is making an effort. Be a leader in the cause — you may influence countless others to follow your example.

26. Eat to Help the Earth.

Some of the most potent environmental offenders are huge factory farms, which generate massive waste and pollution and put large amounts of chemicals into the ground, water, and air. What a cruelty to the earth! To help offset this earth-destroying institution, and to vote with your dollars for kinder treatment of the animals we use for food, revamp the way you eat. Buy organic food whenever you can. Visit the local farmers' market and get your food from small family farms. Organic food used to be expensive, but it is becoming much more affordable, and food at farmers' markets and farm stands is often cheaper than conventionally produced food at the supermarket. Grow a garden in your yard or in containers on your porch or balcony. Compost your food waste. Whether you have a big outdoor composter or a bucket under your sink to collect food scraps to take to your town's compost site, you can use the resulting compost in your own garden or on your potted plants. Eat less meat and fewer dairy products, and when you do eat them, choose organic products or those produced by small family-owned or local farms and dairies. Eat more vegetables. Vegetables, especially when freshly picked, are better for your health. All these actions send a message to those in charge that you are voting with your dollars for more naturally produced food.

27. Rethink Your Transportation.

Vehicle emissions cause a lot of air pollution, with consequences to the humans who breathe the air and the livability of the earth itself. To be kinder to the earth, drive less and ride your bike more, or take public transportation more often. Carpool — you'll reduce emissions and build connections with your fellow riders. And when it's time to get a new vehicle, consider an electric or hybrid car.

28. Live Greener.

Wasting precious resources when others are in need is not just unkind but irresponsible. Whenever you choose not to waste something, it frees up more (whether directly or indirectly) for those who have less. Also, less trash and lower energy use help preserve the earth, making you a better steward of your environment and extending a kindness to the future generations who will live here. Even little things can make a difference over time, so be conscious of wasting electricity and water, and use only what you need. Turn off the lights at night and when you leave a room. Shut down computers when they're not in use. Set the thermostat lower in winter, higher in summer. Consider adding insulation to save on energy expenditure and installing solar panels or wind power, if you live in an area where these alternative energy sources are available and sensible. Become more conscious of the solid waste you produce and see if you can reduce it. Buy food in bulk to reduce packaging. Buy less and throw less away — fix or reuse things instead of buying new; or buy things used. Use organic lawn care products and cleaning products in your home. See if you can live more simply to reduce consumption. Not only do these things help the earth, but they allow you to feel cleaner, calmer, and more at ease about your life.

29. Turn Your Vacation into a Volunteer or Mission Trip.

Instead of sitting on a beach or spending money in a big city, consider taking a solo, couple, or family vacation that also does something good for others. Mission trips or volunteer vacations go all over the world, and are becoming more popular; many organizations offer them. Some are managed by religious organizations, but others are purely secular, with a humanitarian focus. You and your family might end up cleaning trails in national parks; caring for rescued wildlife; cleaning up trash on land or in the ocean; aiding communities hit by natural disasters; or helping small villages in developing countries construct buildings or dig wells or plant gardens.

30. When Disaster Strikes, Volunteer Time, Aid, or Money.

Whether they are hurricanes, tornados, floods, wildfires, landslides, or earthquakes, natural disasters destroy lives. You can always donate money to organizations such as the Red Cross, or go yourself, if you are able (and the local authorities allow it). During Hurricane Katrina, many people traveled to the affected area to help with cleanup and rebuilding, to collect pets separated from their owners, or to bring truckloads of food and supplies to those affected. Man-made crises can create disastrous situations, too — when gatherings turn into riots, when schools experience shootings, or when buildings or other structures collapse, harming hundreds, the affected communities experience deep crisis and mourning, and can use support from others. It can make a big difference to them to know that people from other communities around the country are stepping up to help. So, the next time there is a natural disaster or a man-made crisis, think about what you can do, either from afar or directly, if you are able, to send a message that people care.

31. Shift Your Holidays.

Instead of giving to people who already have enough, consider donating everything you would have spent during the holiday season to a cause you believe in. There are many opportunities to do this. You could sponsor a child in someone's name or donate to a cause each person on your gift list supports. There are organizations that specifically perform these functions.

Donations go toward the gift of school for children; of food, farm animals, or wells for poor communities so that they can become more independent. (Do your research to be sure the organization is a good one and that the money and other resources actually reach the people who need them.) Some families spend Thanksgiving dinner volunteering at a soup kitchen, or play Santa by anonymously delivering presents, Christmas trees, and food to families who can't afford them. If you do buy presents, think about what you buy. Look for gifts that are made by local artists, or food products (for example, chocolate and coffee) that are "fair trade," meaning all those in the supply chain were fairly treated and fairly paid. Or buy items produced by people in other countries who are guaranteed to get a percentage of the proceeds (for example, handmade textiles or jewelry).

32. Help to Shape the next Generation.

Everything you do for kids is something you do for the future. These are the people who will be running the world a few decades down the line. Find ways to make their formative experiences more oriented toward future good. Like Fred Rogers, who was so gifted at building self-esteem in children by listening and affirming their uniqueness, you, too, can help children gain confidence and feel more secure in who they are. If you have kids, set an example. Be the person you would like to see them be in the future. Remember that children learn what they live and are more likely to do what you do than what you say. If your actions don't match your words, they will notice. Teach them to be kind in all the ways you seek to be kind. Point it out to them. Talk about it. Ask for their ideas.

If you don't have children, or if your children are already grown up, get involved anyway, just a little, or a lot. Talk to the neighborhood kids. See what their lives are like. Offer help where you can. Be a good listener. Be friendly and tell them what you appreciate about them. Or, your influence could be more structured: volunteer to tutor or read to kids, or offer your own special skills at a local youth organization or recreation center. Support your local schools, either financially or with your time. Can you help in the library? With after-school care? On the national level, contribute to causes that help children receive education, better health care, and better support. "Children are the future" sounds cliché, but nothing could be truer. If you want the future world to be kinder, help children become kinder, better people, and that is what will happen.

ACKNOWLEDGMENTS: THANK YOU, KINDLY!

Thank you to Joe Campbell, Bob Marty, and Linda Simensky. Because of our conversation about how kindness is the through-line of every one of the shows I've ever created, I've had the opportunity to write this book. Kindness is at the foundation of my life's work. I'm a child advocate, so my vision has been to change and use media to give back to the next generation. I want children to feel empowered, challenged, and kind. I want to make sure that we showcase the very best curriculum on every show I create. I may create shows that teach kindergarten readiness skills (*Blue's Clues*), reading (*Super Why!*), social and emotional life lessons (*Daniel Tiger's Neighborhood*), the arts (*Creative Galaxy*), executive functioning skills (*Wishenpoof*), and story-telling (*Charlie's Colorforms City*). But above all else, our characters, our storylines, and our themes all embody kindness.

Exploring and diving deep into the radicalness of kindness and truly understanding its power has me wanting to scream it from the rooftops. What an honor and thrill it has been to have the opportunity to share my passions with you in this book. It has been a gift to me, and I hope it's been a gift for you, too!

I would like to thank those in my world who have been truly kind to me. Those who have seen me through their hearts and seen the real me. Year after year, I've been able to peel back the layers of myself and be out in the world without my armor. Because of your kindness, I have been able to be silly, creative, and strategic, and even to have the courage to make radical ideas come true. Thank you!

To Bob Marty, thank you for being a true innovator and creative producer on this beautiful project. I hope we change the world, together!

To my husband, Gregory: You were the first person to truly see me. The depth of your kindness has swept me off my feet, and you do it all without any fanfare. You are one of a kind. To my daughters, Hope and Ella, I see all of you with my heart and couldn't love you any more than I do. Your kindness to others and to the world continues to motivate me.

To Alex Glass for being a wonderful literary agent and partner. To Eve Adamson, thank you for working in the trenches with me, helping me to dig deeper, and believing in my message. To Dean Winchester, thank you for being *you.* You are my hero. To Maura Poston Zagrans, thank you, kindly, for your work. To everyone at Harper Wave who supported my mission and vision: Karen Rinaldi, Hannah Robinson, and Rebecca Raskin.

To the amazing Deepak Chopra for his words of wisdom — you have been an inspiration to me for as long as I can remember. Thank you for being so kind. To Marty Robinson, Richard Wiese, Greg Young, Dr. Taz, Dr. Suzuki, Ken Burns, Gretchen Rubin, Dr. Brené Brown, and my fellow Harrington Park Elementary School and Old Tappan High School friend, Senator Cory Booker. Your words have been a kind gift to me, and to our country. Thank you for continuing to inspire us all.

To everyone on our amazing

9 Story USA staff — Wendy Harris, Marcy Pritchard, Alex Breen, Rachel Kalban, Sarah Wallendjack, Shevaun Grey, Alexandra Cassel, Steph Cleaver Six, Gord Garwood, Kyra Halperin, Maddie Kroll, Hailey Grier, Aly Piekarsky, Noriko Louison, Maddy Feiner, Jill Cozza Turner, Rebecca Plaut, Chelsea Kramer, and Taryn Campbell: You are the most passionate and kindest people I know; you work every day to make the world a better place for kids.

To everyone at 9 Story Media Group and Brown Bag Films, most especially Vince Commisso — thank you for your leadership and your vision of what we can do for kids, the world, and our business.

Always remember, "Let it fuel your Italian fire . . ." To Natalie Osborne, Cathal Gaffney, Darragh O'Connor, and Blake Tohana — thank you for being my wonderfully supportive, strategic, and creative team. To all of our amazing directors, producers, and animators, namely Vadim, Tanya, Bill, Julie, Tammy, Cory, Paula, and the Voodoo Highway team. To Jen Hamburg and Becky Friedman Lowitt — wherever you go, I will follow! Thank you for always having just the *kind* thing to say.

To DHX, with Phillip, Jay, Colleen, Anne, and all the creatives at DHX Halifax, including Blain Morris, for your musical genius.

To my best friend and co-creator

of my first show, *Blue's Clues,* Traci Paige Johnson: You are one of the kindest souls I have ever met; you want only what's best for everyone around you. You taught me the importance of sharpening the saw and how much I need to belly-laugh with you. To Dr. Alice Wilder, thank you for doing what you do for kids every day. To the *BC* OGs! Steve Burns, Donovan Patton, Jeremy Slutskin, Dave Palmer, Marcy Pritchard, Jonathan Judge, Jennifer Twomey, as well as Traci, Wendy, and Alice. To our new "cousin," Joshua Dela Cruz, you are going to hit it out of the park and be every preschooler's best friend!

To my friends at Nickelodeon, Sarah Landy — what would we do without you? Cathy Galeota, Kim Rosenblum, Pam Kaufman, and Chris Viscardi. To PBS Kids, in particular Paula Kerger, Lesli Rotenberg, Sara DeWitt, and especially Linda Simensky. To Fred Rogers Productions, especially Paul Siefken, Kevin Morrison, Chris Loggins, Ellen Dougherty, and Bill Isler. To Amazon Kids, with Michelle Sullivan and Melissa Wolfe. And to everyone at Netflix, especially Dominique Bazay and Josh Fisher; and to everyone at Apple, especially Tara Sorenson. You have all made my dreams come true!

To my research mentors: Dr. Rosemarie Truglio, Dr. Herb Ginsburg at Teachers College, Columbia University; Dr. Dan Anderson at

UMass — you have all been an unbelievable source of inspiration. To Gerry Laybourne — it is so kind of you to spend so much time with me as we continue to innovate for kids. To Kit Laybourne — you gave me my first "break"; interning for you was one of my greatest gifts. To Stacey Levin, your smarts, creativity, and strategic thinking are unparalleled. Plus, you make me laugh! To my CUA family for showing me the way. To my friends in Anguilla, especially Peter and Anne Parles at Straw Hat. To Marc Chamlin, for your smarts; John Tishbe, for your expertise. For Ellen Galinsky, friend and author of the groundbreaking book *Mind in the Making;* and Diane Tracy, friend and author of *Blue's Clues for Success* — so happy to be working with you. To my seventh-grade English teacher, Andy Walker.

To my beautiful, loud, and fun-loving Italian American family: my mom, Mary Jane Capobianco, for teaching me how to be kind yet strong and independent; my dad, for teaching me how to be strategic; my brother, Robert, for asking a lot of questions and inspiring me; my sister, Jennifer, for being my first best friend. To Alicia, Dawn, RAJ, Vinnie, Francesca, and Chris — you have my heart. My cousins Felicia, Jim, Christine, Lori, Julie, Gabriella, Elizabeth, and Peter — my visits with you make me so happy. To all the Santomeros, especially my mother-in-law and father-in-law, Lauretta and Vinny — you always believed in me, and it was your kindnesses that made me reach for the stars. To all the kids in my life who grew up on my shows: Morgan, Perry (from our very first *Blue's Clues* mail time letter), Sabrina, Jenna (my Paprika and Muffin Pan), Beau, Austin, Ryan, Grant, Will, Meri, Jack, Christopher, Calista, Landon, Aidan, Peter, Reese, Bennett, Vivian, Meadow, and Levi.

For my friends: Deb Reber (coauthor of my first book), your support and kindness means the world to me; to Rachel, you stood up for me when we were twelve, and I was forever changed by your act of kindness; Joyce and Alyssa, your friendship is a gift to me. To Joanne Rogers, thank you for being my friend; you are a light in my life.

And of course, to Fred Rogers, for being my mentor. You started it all, and children's media thanks you for it.

ABOUT THE AUTHOR

Angela C. Santomero is the co-creator of the award-winning *Blue's Clues* and the creator of the smash hits *Daniel Tiger's Neighborhood; Creative Galaxy* and *Wishenpoof;* and *Charlie's Colorforms City.* The chief creative officer of 9 Story Media Group, she is the recipient of a Peabody Award, two Television Critics Association Awards, and the 2018 World Screen's Kids Trend-setter Award. She has been nominated for more than twenty-five Emmy Awards and numerous Parents' Choice Gold and Silver Awards. Angela is the author of *Preschool Clues* and blogs on AngelasClues.com. She lives in New York with her husband, two daughters, and two puppies.

The employees of Thorndike Press hope you have enjoyed this Large Print book. All our Thorndike, Wheeler, and Kennebec Large Print titles are designed for easy reading, and all our books are made to last. Other Thorndike Press Large Print books are available at your library, through selected bookstores, or directly from us.

For information about titles, please call:
(800) 223-1244

or visit our website at:
gale.com/thorndike

To share your comments, please write:
Publisher
Thorndike Press
10 Water St., Suite 310
Waterville, ME 04901